Cartwheels on the Curbside

A Memoir

Kenneth Strange

To Brandon,
for allowing me to fully be myself.

Discovery Park. Seattle, WA. July 2020

KENNETH STRANGE

Contents

Preface

Adam Whitaker is a composite character. I disguised this person's identity and specific details of their involvement as my coach at King County Gymnastics to honor their complete privacy. Their participation in my life story is that they coached me, made an indelible impact, and then moved away. That is all I will share. The real-life Adam Whitaker is one of the best coaches I have ever been mentored by. Their influence is the main reason for much of the success I experienced as a gymnast and in my coaching, even today.

Asher Yosef is a composite character drawn from several men who were discipling me at various times and locations throughout my time in the International Churches of Christ.

The following are pseudonyms: Jennette, Chuck, Megan, Joel, Melanie, Kip, Susan, Walker, Abel, Chelsea, Jessica, Anders, Mirabel, Parker, Alarik Sachs, Chad Lopez, Aleksandr Sokolov, Charles Langford, Mitch Marseilles, Owen, Julian, James, Ivan, Jacob & Sarah Boseman, Joshua, Amir, Jillian, Mrs. X, Elina, Zeke, EJ, Elite Gymnastics Academy, Lilac City Gymnastics, Mount Lake Terrace Gymnastics Academy, King County Gymnastics,

Post Falls International Church of Christ, and Mercer Island International Church of Christ. Additionally, all church locations have been changed.

The earliest depictions of my parents do not represent who they are today. They no longer subscribe to homophobic sentiments. Further, I acknowledge that I was a horrendously difficult child to raise. They did their best to bring me up strong and independent. I am grateful for who they are today and the love they have shown me in my adulthood.

I intend no harm to the real-life persons, churches, and gymnastics clubs described throughout this book. I wish the real-life members of the ICOC peace as they navigate their spiritual journeys. Many fine members are in the movement, and I recognize that their memories of events and depictions described in this book are likely different from mine.

A Note from the Author

In 1993, the International Churches of Christ was considered one of the fastest-growing church organizations in the country. ABC's 20/20 underwent an undercover investigation into the tactics of the church. Barbara Walters noted that many former members were publicly coming forward with dramatic stories of coercion and brainwashing before posing the question: Is the International Churches of Christ a cult?

"Well," she said, "that depends on whom you ask. Thousands say it has changed their lives for the better."

When I joined the church twenty years after the interview aired, I believed it had changed my life. Today, I am a former member, and this is my story.

The names and identifying characteristics of some persons described in this book have been changed. While all the incidents described in this book are true, certain events have been compressed, consolidated, or reordered to protect the identities of the people involved and ensure the continuity of the narrative. All dialogue has been recreated to the best of my recollection.

Prologue

I wanted the assurance of salvation. But it was also my fourth time romanticizing falling in love. I was walking across the 130th Street bridge overlooking Interstate 5. Sometimes, I'd glorify that, too. You know, jumping off. I didn't understand why it felt so unobtainable—living as a disciple of Jesus. Why some people in the organization could make it look so effortless was beyond me.

The longer I lived as a disciple, the more difficult it became to keep going. Entertaining the thought of leaving on my own volition made me anxious. Entertaining the idea of mentally checking out because I didn't have the strength to live faithfully frightened me even more. Because that meant I was lost, which told me my salvation was at risk. Most nights, I'd struggle to fall asleep because of the stress. Then, after viewing something on my phone that I probably shouldn't have, I'd wake up the next day and confess my shortcomings to my discipler. It felt like that's all I'd been doing—confessing sins and daydreaming about running away.

But then I found the 20/20 documentary on YouTube. This was the beginning of the end of my discipleship. Or so I thought.

Hillyard

Spokane

Cartwheels on the Curbside

My first memories of the sport come from a picture tucked away in the family photo album on the bottom shelf of my mom's vitrine. A blanket of dust now rests evenly across several elephant trinkets, and a picture frame—housing my mother's 1980s glamour shot—perched on the top ledge. I glance briefly at Mom's smile before crouching to grab the maroon-colored album decorated in Autumn florals. As a kid, I frequently found myself thumbing through the tattered album, always stopping to examine a picture of me donning a vampire cape. In the photo, I'm standing in Berney Elementary's Library, the school I attended when my family lived in Walla Walla, Washington.

My face looks washed out from the quality of the disposable camera. Everyone in the background is marching in a circle around the library. Some kids dressed as clowns, others as muscle men, but almost every kid carried a stuffed animal, likely to exhibit animal-taming skills. At the tail end of the photograph, the quiet kid, whose name I don't remember, looks in the direction of the camera, a clown smile and nose painted on his face, dressed in a long-sleeved shirt tucked into jean pants, his expression—uncertain, perhaps relaxed.

The production resembled a Kidz Bop version of a Cirque Du Soleil show. I could see pom-poms and confetti, smell popcorn wafting around the scent of used books, and overheating desktop computers. About fifteen kindergartners talked and laughed while Fatboy Slim's *Praise You* played through two giant speakers on the floor.

"If you're listening and you know it, clap your hands!" Mrs. K sang out to garner our attention.

Clap Clap!

"Good afternoon, parents, and good afternoon, boys and girls! Welcome to the Berney Kindergarten Annual Circus Show!" Her voice echoed through the speakers as she held onto a piece of paper and a microphone in the same hand.

Usually, I disliked going to the library. It always felt like a quiet and dull space for teachers to chat academically with students learning to build sentences or summarize chapters. Now, the atmosphere appeared more to my satisfaction—chaos. Earlier in the week, Mrs. K spent an afternoon teaching us about animals by assigning the class a color-by-number page associated with the circus. However, Mrs. K wasted her lesson on me because I could have passed as one. She often reprimanded me for running around the classroom or jumping off tables. Untreated ADHD and a level of oppositional defiance characterized my early childhood education. Whenever I became too challenging, Mrs. K brought me to sit in the "thinking room," a dimly lit closet-sized space with a bean bag chair and a small desk.

A small viewing window at the top of the door let in light from the hallway outside. It also allowed Mrs. K and the school administrators to observe those who, like me, sat inside. I became a Think Time regular, always stimming on the bean bag chair or drawing pictures at the desk. Sometimes, the admin entered the room with me, and we'd talk about my drawings. I often scribbled my rendition of the Teletubbies, each character meticulously lined in a row, colored accordingly— Purple for Tinkiwinki, light green for Dipsi, yellow for LaLa, and red for Po.

My hyperactive, attention-seeking behavior landed me the role of an acrobat in the circus show. I later learned I'd partake in a partner performance shared by Quiet Kid, who stood across the circle from me. Mrs. K insisted I dress with everyone else so I wouldn't miss out on all the fun, but I winced at the idea of wearing a costume. Did I hate playing pretend, or did I feel jealous of everyone's confidence to assume a character? I can't say for sure. But my sister, Michele, lent me her vampire cape from Halloween. Since she felt courageous enough to wear it, so did I.

"Alright, boys and girls! Follow me!" Mrs. K announced.

Everyone began marching around the library, following Mrs. K's lead. As I followed the kid in front of me, my attention wandered to the silver and gold tassel jutting out of yellow and orange stepping stools librarians use to reach the books on high shelves.

I felt jittery, but the bright colors and sparkles were a suitable distraction. I glanced at Mrs. K for direction, who guided everyone to their places. I began understanding my role when she pulled Quiet Kid and me aside and paired us as tightrope walkers. The room fell silent. Mrs. K pointed to a duct tape square on the carpet.

"Kenny, come stand here." I could hear her call Quiet Kid over to a second small duct tape platform connected to mine by a longer piece. "Feast your eyes on the incredible! On one side, you'll see Kenny the Magnificent and on the other, you'll see Quiet Kid the Great!" She belted with a cheap baritone voice. Did she attempt to impersonate a carnival barker? "Get ready as this dynamic duo begins to climb the ladder in front of them!"

I looked over to Mrs. K; she mimed climbing a ladder, still holding the microphone plugged into one of the speakers. The paper in her hand slipped out and fell to the floor. Quiet Kid and I began climbing the make-believe ladder in front of us.

"They have made their way to the top of the platform! You're all in for a real treat this afternoon! What tricks do these gentlemen have in store?"

She looked at Quiet Kid and rolled her arms forward to mime a somersault across the duct tape. He stood tall, reached for the sky, and then rolled across the duct tape, using his hands to push himself back to his feet while the audience cheered for him. How did he know to somersault? Did we practice this before?

Feeling nervous and unsure how to set myself apart from Quiet Kid, I pursed my lips, as I'd seen Michele do before, to show everyone I looked ready and focused; they'd see me as the real star of this show. I reached tall like Quiet Kid and rolled across the duct tape after him. A round of applause echoed through the library. I got back onto my feet and reached tall again. Mrs. K continued to play along with a hint of uncertainty in her voice. "What's this? Does Kenny the Magnificent have another trick for us?"

I placed my hands on the ground, kicking my feet into the air sideways before falling. Did it look like the cartwheel I intended to accomplish or like an elephant jumping in circles? Despite toppling over, everyone clapped for me. Whatever humiliation I felt, my parents drowned out by their standing ovation. Quiet Kid and I bowed to the audience before marching back into the crowd of children. And then, I'd close the photo album and remember the scene differently.

I don't have a concrete memory of the circus performance; only fragmented scenes attached to several reimagined plots framed around my childhood hopes of becoming a U.S. Olympic gymnast remain. Over the years, I likely recreated and expanded the memories accompanying the photograph.

My interest in pursuing gymnastics materialized the following year. While running around during lunch recess, I noticed a girl who could run into a round-off back handspring on the grass. Witnessing a round-off back handspring is all it took to set my love for the sport into motion.

"Woah!" I yelled. "How did you do that?"

Jennette Taylor paused for a moment, examining me. "I'm in gymnastics!" she responded as if to question how surprised I was.

"Oh! Well, could you teach me how to do that, too?"

"Um no!" she retorted, maintaining a snarky tone.

She looked to her friend Megan, who rolled her eyes and scoffed.

"Please?" I begged.

"No! Now leave me alone!"

Over the years, Jennette and I would go on to share moments of friendship and civility, only to become nemeses again hours later. She would act pleasant to me in the morning but turn uptight by the afternoon. Jennette's bright eyes sparkled, and her long blond hair—curled perfectly so—seemed to emit a colorful aura attracting everyone to her. She almost always treated me like dirt, and I hated her for it. At the same time, I sought after her alliance. Because of her beauty, I wanted to clothe myself in her look and style. By the time we reached the fourth grade, we grew only a few decibels short of sworn enemies. She trained as a competitive gymnast at a local club, and I did not.

Dad would never allow that. It didn't fit his vision for me. I knew this but attempted to persuade him as often as possible. "Why can't I take gymnastics classes?"

"Because Kenny," he'd say, not looking up from the football game on T.V. "Gymnastics is for girls."

"Please, Dad! I want to take gymnastics!"

"No."

"Please?"

"Kenny!" He'd snapped his fingers, pointing at me. "No son of mine will be in a sissy sport like gymnastics!"

"Fine! I'm never speaking to you again!"

"Oh, please! Don't threaten me with a good time!" Dad continued sarcastically, "Now run, fly, be free."

Despite Dad's disapproval, I managed ways to entertain my goals for gymnastics. My friend Joel and I met in the second grade in Mrs. W's class and hit it off instantly. We were incredibly chatty with one another and often got separated for wasting time. One afternoon, while playing alone in the alley behind my house, I discovered Joel lived on the same street as me. I spotted him walking his dog along Morton Street at the cross-section where our alleys separated.

"Joel?"

"Hey, Kenny!" He said, grunting, as his dog tried pulling him away. "Stop, Gumdrop!"

"Where do you live?"

Joel pointed east toward his alley. "Follow me, and I'll show you! You can meet my mom!"

When I stepped onto his property, I knew I wanted to spend all my free time at his house because he seemed to have everything a kid could want. As we entered his backyard, he boasted a giant trampoline. I thought he was rich. His bedroom looked equally impressive. He had a Power Rangers bedspread and a working telephone beside a T.V. with Comcast cable on top of an entertainment center. Dad only bought a cable subscription for the living room, and he usually got control of the T.V. Joel also owned several gaming consoles: PlayStation, Xbox, and even a Gameboy. But none of those heightened my senses like his trampoline. I only experienced jumping on a trampoline one other time before. I bounced around his yard with giddy anticipation to leverage it to overcome my fears of doing a back handspring like Jennette. However, I first needed a permission slip signed by Dad. Once I obtained the note from Dad, Joel and I embarked on an adventure to learn a backflip together.

We spent several weeks practicing to no avail. We couldn't overcome our fears. But then Joel approached me one day after school while walking home. "I can do a backflip now!"

I turned to him. "Dude. No, you can't."

"Bet me! Come over later, and I'll show you!"

I refused to believe it until I saw it with my own eyes. Joel invited me to a sleepover a few nights before. The likelihood he learned a backflip in that short time seemed improbable. But I watched him jump on the trampoline with his friend Kip, backflipping as if he'd done the skill his whole life. Kip, who never treated me nicely, alternated backflips with Joel. It felt like they were intentionally taunting me.

I stood in the alley, jealously watching them accomplish what felt impossible. "Oh, dude! No way! You gotta teach me that!"

Kip stopped jumping and looked over at me. "Dude. Go away! Nobody wants you here!"

"Joel does! He's my friend. Tell him, Joel!"

"Maybe come back later. Me and Kip are hanging out now."

The two of them pitted themselves against me, so I walked home. Kip was a few years older, so I understood. I would have done the same thing to Joel. He'd become my friend again once Kip left. When we weren't jumping on the trampoline, we hung out in his bedroom watching T.V. or pretended a kidnapper lurked outside his window to steal us in the night. "Kids! We're coming to get you!" One of us would say in a shrieking voice before giggling while pulling the blankets over our faces. Joel's mom, Melanie, became like a second mom to me. During sleepovers, Melanie would cook breakfast. She'd make eggs, bacon, toast, and our choice of drink, either hot chocolate or orange juice.

"Brunch is ready!" She called out.

I walked into the kitchen, unsure what she meant, and asked, "What is brunch?"

Melanie handed me a breakfast plate. "It's the period after breakfast but before lunch! It's like a casual weekend meal when you don't have to stick to a schedule."

I didn't know a name existed to describe it.

Life at Joel's felt like a night-and-day difference from my life at home. I wasn't as connected to my family as how I saw Joel with his mom. Money always seemed tight. The reason I received fewer cool electronics than Joel. I could go without the material objects as long as I could learn a backflip properly in a gymnastics class. However, gymnastics classes weren't an option. Dad insisted I'd want to play football once I got to high school.

On a calm summer afternoon, I stood beside Dad as he arranged some briquettes for the barbecue. He lowered a burning piece of paper into the charcoal. "Don't you want to play football like your old man?"

"No, I don't." I squatted to pet my cat, Z.Z., who wandered past, likely on his way to knock up more of the neighborhood female cats. "Doesn't sound fun at all."

I could feel the heat from the fire as the flames rose, tufts of smoke swirling up. Dad sat in the lawn chair as our neighbor Susan and her three kids, Walker, Abel, and Chelsea, filtered into the backyard.

Dad looked back at me. "It's a lot of fun!"

I kneeled beside him. "It's boring and stupid. I want to learn cool flips and tricks!"

"Well, that won't be happening... But I still love you!"

I hated when Dad added, "But I still love you!" at the end of an argument because he always said it with a sarcastic emphasis. I always interpreted it as a "fuck you!"

"But Dad!"

"But nothing, Kenny. You don't see Walker or Abel wanting to do gymnastics, do you?"

"No..." I sighed. "Well, can I at least get a big trampoline?"

"Those are like a hundred dollars. I'm not spending money on something that will get broken and discarded in a few months."

"Please, Joel has one, and I want one, too!"

"Well, you can go jump at Joel's!"

"It's not the same, and you know that."

"I know... but I still love you!"

Fuck you too, Dad!

"But—"

"Go play with the boys."

"Dad!"

He shooed me away. "Now, Run, fly, be free!"

At school, whenever I was near Jennette, I thought she and I would become full-time friends if I made a competitive gymnastics team. She looked stunning. Her athletic prowess and intelligence made her ooze with unparalleled confidence. I assumed her majestic nature filled the room *because* she took gymnastics. Jennette exuded talent, surrounded herself with a vibrant friend group, possessed academic ambition, and had supportive parents to help guide her. I wet the bed, wore the same clothes, publicly picked my nose, and gave next to zero effort in the classroom, but I desperately wanted to look cool. I lied to Jennette, hoping to impress her. "I'm in gymnastics now!"

She glanced at me. "Oh? Where?"

I knew the name of the gym Jennette attended, so I rattled off a different name I found in the phonebook. "Lilac City Gymnastics."

"Oh, Lilac City?" She said, making it seem like the wrong choice of gym. "They're our rival!"

"Well, I like it. I'm learning so much!"

The only gymnastics training I did amounted to whatever time I spent on Joel's trampoline trying to learn a backflip with his guidance. But he immensely helped because I eventually got the skill. I believed if I could learn to backflip, I could learn anything. I felt uninterested, sheepish even, to participate in most sports. During P.E., I secretly hoped our teacher, Mrs. C, would involve our class in a weekly gymnastics lesson as she did for sports like basketball. I refused to participate in activities that didn't resonate with me. Once, in the sixth grade, my class took a trip to launch rockets we designed for a science project. During my group's intermission at the park, while we waited for another group to finish their session, Mrs. S gathered everyone for a quick kickball game.

"Kenny, you're on deck to kick," Mrs. S said as I sat in the dugout.

"I don't want to play."

"Yes. Everyone must kick at least once."

"No, I'm not!" I said before dramatically running away.

Two girls from my class ran after me, at Mrs. S's request, to make sure I stayed within a reasonable distance.

"Why don't you want to play? It's a lot of fun!" One of the girls asked sympathetically.

"Because I can't! My gymnastics teacher said I'm not allowed to!" I screamed, with tears running off my chin.

"Well, tell Mrs. S that. I'm sure she'll understand."

Mrs. S didn't buy it. "No, your gymnastics instructor did not say that! Everybody will kick the ball at least one time, including you."

"No, I'm not, and you can't make me!"

After about a minute of resistance, the rest of the class, who wanted the game to continue, began yelling at me to play. "Kick the ball so the rest of us can continue playing!"

"No!"

"Oh my God!" I heard Jennette yell out. "Kick the ball!"

I viewed all sports involving a ball as manly—the last adjective I wanted to assimilate into. My interests were umbrellas, Easy Bake Ovens, High School Musical, the Spice Girls, and, more recently, the porn DVD stash hidden underneath Dad's side of the bed. Early on, I learned that my interests differed from boys my age. Mom and Dad often compared my masculinity, or lack thereof, to Walker's. They always reminded me what my assigned gender role in society was.

"You're a boy—It's time to start acting like one!"

They wanted me to imitate Walker. Instead, I would practice my cartwheels along the curbside in front of my house, eliciting words of humiliation from anybody who might've watched me, usually in the form of a question: "Why is Kenny so gay?" Homosexuality wasn't a topic positively discussed at home, only brought forth disparagingly during political discussions. I don't remember who said it first; perhaps Dad or one of his buddies from work. I heard the statement repeated so often it became seared into my conscience. "Faggots don't need rights. It's fucking disgusting. We don't need to see that shit in public!"

"What does that mean?" I once asked.

"It's when two dudes jump on one another and do something nasty."

"Why is it bad?"

"Because it's against God and nature."

I made a point to agree with homophobic sentiments audibly, "Oh, gross!"

But I also felt in tune with myself, keenly aware the sight of a shirtless man piqued my interest enough to give me a raging erection.

A Real Lady's Man

Her neighbor looked like a tired garden gnome smoking a cigarette on his porch steps. He held a beer bottle in his hand as a thick glob of phlegm avalanched his chin to his wrist, unfazed by his appearance.

"Who's that?" I asked.

"Eww!" Lynn yelled audibly enough for him to hear. "That's Rusty! Now listen! You stay away from him. He's nasty!"

"Okay, I will. Is there anything to do here? I'm bored."

"Well, I can put a movie on! I rented The Lion King from Blockbuster! You wanna go inside and watch it, squirt?"

"Do you have Scream?"

"Scream? You're not old enough to watch scary movies!"

"Yes, I am. I'm five! I like it. It's spooky."

"Uh, no. If your dad lets you watch it, fine, but I won't!"

The garden gnome stood up, hacked a few coughs before tossing his cigarette butt onto the pavement. He lingered outside his doorstep momentarily before slipping into the dark unit, locking his eyes with Lynn as he shut the door.

"He is sick, Kenny."

"He is?"

"I don't want you going anywhere near that man, got it?" she said, "anyway, I don't have Scream. I have The Lion King. I heard you love it. Whadya say? Wanna watch it with me?"

"Okay."

We only watched twenty minutes of the movie when we heard a knock at the door. Lynn walked over. "Hi, Chuck! Come on in."

She waltzed into the living room and paused the film. "Chuck, this is my son, Kenny!"

Chuck stepped forward. "Nice to meet you, little buddy!"

I didn't respond, unsure of the strange man.

Lynn continued looking at me. "Kenny, do you have anything to say back?"

Silence.

She slapped the top of her T.V. "Stop acting like the little shit like your father teaches you to be. Say hi back to the man, for Christ's sake!"

More silence.

"Okay, kid," She rolled her eyes while lighting a cigarette. "We're going to the backroom for a while. Don't disturb us for any reason, got it?"

I finally spoke up, "Do you have any crayons?"

Lynn stood halfway between her bedroom door and the living room.

"I don't know," she said softly. Her voice cracked as she motioned Chuck into the kitchen. "Will you check the drawer next to the fridge to see if there's anything for my son to color with?"

Chuck pulled out a broken white crayon.

"I can't color with this!" I protested.

"Well, sure you can!" he said, marking the paper.

"You can't see it!"

He shrugged. "You'll make it work."

They walked into the back bedroom, leaving me with the broken white crayon and The Lion King to babysit until the end of our visitation. I could see why Dad and Lynn didn't get along. Lynn was supposedly my second mom, but Mom and Dad talked trash about her. They would claim she's irresponsible and unfit to be a mother. In response, Lynn would say that Dad gave her herpes. Dad ensured I knew she wasn't my mother when I wasn't around her. "Lynn is only your birth mom. She doesn't love you like your real mom does."

He often referred to Lynn as the "bio-woman." I'd kick, shout, and plead, but Dad remained adamant I spend a few hours bonding with her. Between Dad and Lynn, there were always two competing stories taking place. Whenever I entered Lynn's apartment, she said I couldn't use her name. She insisted I call her mom. Everything about my time with Lynn felt forced and unnatural. We got into petty arguments frequently during our visits.

"My mommy is Debbie! And she lives with me! You're not my real mommy!" I shouted during one of our more turbulent visits.

"Oh, please. Kid, I'm the one who gave birth to you! Your dad and Debbie STOLE you away from me!"

"That's not what my dad said! He said you didn't want me!"

"Bullshit, kid! Your dad's a liar!"

"Take me home now!"

Lynn flew into hysterics. "You know what? Fine! I will!"

She paced through her apartment while lighting a cigarette. She grabbed her keys and, though it was the middle of summer, her coat and stomped her feet into a pair of flip-flops. Suddenly, I felt her grab me by the wrist. She treaded headlong across Emma Street, dragging me behind. When we arrived at my house, she gently nudged me onto the steps to knock three times on the mahogany.

My brother, Justin, opened the door, and seeing me, he walked into his adjacent bedroom.

"Here you go, Deb and Wes," Lynn shouted from the sidewalk below, "you win! He's YOUR KID!"

"I don't ever want to see you ever again!" I screamed back.

"Fine!"

"Fine!"

I imagine Michele came over and closed the door. Mom and Dad were likely shopping at the Super 1 Foods behind our house that afternoon. Because my earliest memories are only vague images, half-remembered, the fill-in-the-blank portion is an invention of my imagination. Only after my family left Walla Walla do my memories come into focus.

We moved to Spokane, Washington, in 2000 and settled in a little gray house at 1028 E. Bridgeport Avenue. Across the street, two houses to the left toward Nevada Street, a Pizza Hut stands on the corner; we sometimes ordered takeout. To the south on Morton Street, Gonzaga Prep High School sits at the base of the hill. Longfellow Elementary, where I would attend in the Fall, resides only a few blocks north, off Nevada and Providence Avenue. I spent my afternoons directly after school or in the summertime running amok with the neighborhood kids. We'd ride our bikes to swim at the Hillyard Aquatic Center or explore the backwoods of

Beacon Hill. But most often, we gathered on the football field at Gonzaga Prep.

Once, when I was eleven, a small group of shirtless college guys tossed a football around while their girlfriends walked the track.

"Go long! Go long! Go long!" I heard in the distance.

Boys my age were taking an interest in girls, but the bodies of the shirtless college guys mid-game caught my eye. I knew I couldn't say anything about it because Walker might suspect I liked men and call me a faggot. Still, I secretly wanted to garner the attention of at least one of the hot guys on the field.

"Look at this, you guys!" I yelled to Walker and Abel. "I can do a roundoff backflip now! No hands! Watch!"

I ran across the turf, hurdled my body into a roundoff, flipped backward like a scorpion midair, and found my feet at the last second. I first landed the flip during Longfellow's talent show. I became encouraged to attempt the skill after watching Jennette land one during her performance. Walker ran over to me.

"How did you figure out how to flip without using your hands at the end?"

"Dude, I don't even know! I ran and did it on one of the blue gymnastics mats during the talent show last night!"

One of the shirtless college guys shouted from a distance, "Eh, yo! That was sick, bro!" while running over to give me a fist bump.

"Thanks, man!"

Beads of sweat on his perfectly chiseled abs plunged onto a trail of hair that grew thicker the further it descended his lower abs. What did he look like below? Speechless and horny, I wondered what would Mom or Dad would think if they knew I got aroused by guys instead of girls. I stood there, staring, as the college guy returned to the inner field.

Walker broke the silence. "What?"

"Nothing." I continued staring. "I hope to have abs like him when I'm older."

"You already have abs, dumbass."

"Oh yeah."

I watched the shirtless guy make a beeline toward his girlfriend to smack her butt before proceeding into the football game.

That summer, my family took a trip to visit my aunt, uncle, and cousins in Walla Walla. It had been almost seven years since I last saw Lynn. She existed now in my memory as a caricature.

"Can we go by the old house? I want to see the old house!" I asked Dad while he drove us around town.

"Sure!"

A Shari's restaurant sat on the plot of land where Lynn's apartment complex once stood.

"They must've moved somewhere else!"

"Only a few miles away! We are on our way to see her now."

"I don't want to go see her."

"That's too bad because we're going to see her."

"Dad—"

"Kenneth David! Not another word! You will be kind. It'll only be an hour, we won't stay long!"

"Ugh, fine!"

We parked in front of her house on 320 N. Roosevelt St, a neglected piece of real estate. On the right-hand side of the house, I saw a dog run. On the left side, I saw dead grass and tall dandelions protruding. On the porch, an ashtray lay next to a worn-out Lazy Boy recliner. I could see cracked linoleum through the screen door with mismatched patterns spread across the floor: roses in one patch and orange and yellow stripes in another. Because most remained, it looked like someone had unsuccessfully tried peeling the top layer to uncover the rose patterns underneath.

"Lynn-ah-do!" Dad called out. "I have a surprise package for you!"

"What? Who? Wha... who's there?" Lynn yelled out, hacking mucus like her old neighbor Rusty did.

"It's me, Wes! Look who I brought to see you."

Dad stepped away from my view, and there she sat on an old couch smoking a cigarette. A box fan blew the smoke out of the window.

"Is that Kenny?" She asked. "Is that my son?"

My heart began pounding so loudly that I thought they could hear the thumping.

Who is this woman?

She looked nothing like how I remembered her. She used to look overly feminine, with make-up done, perfectly manicured nails, and long, curly brown hair. Now, she needed a cane to walk and flaunted a haircut suitable for a butch lesbian woman working in construction.

"Come give your mama a hug!"

I froze.

"Don't be rude," Dad whispered, pushing me toward her. She reeked acrid from the tobacco, and her skin was damp from the warm, stagnant air in the house.

"Come have a seat. Do you want anything to drink?" She asked.

"No, thank you," I responded.

"Well, alright," She pointed to her kitchen. "I have cola in the fridge if you get thirsty. Tell me about you, son! What have you been up to... Y'all are living in Spokane these days, right?"

"Right."

"Well! So, what are your hobbies? You got a girlfriend yet?"

Dad nudged me with his elbow. "He's a real ladies' man, like his old man!"

I looked at Lynn. "I like to do gymnastics."

"Oh? Is that so? Well, that's cool! You learning those cool flips and tricks, squirt?"

"Well, not exactly. My dad won't let me take gymnastics. I only do what I can on my friend's trampoline when I stay at his house."

Lynn swiftly turned to Dad, embodying a thunderstorm off in the distance. "Why won't you put your son in gymnastics?"

Dad teetered his head shoulder to shoulder while shrugging. "Oh... You know it's..."

"It's what, Wes?"

"It's a girl's sport. I don't want him to get bullied for it. We don't have the money for it either."

"Bullshit, Wes!" Lynn yelled. "You and Deb both got jobs. I know you could afford to put him in gymnastics classes if you wanted to. I don't even make half of what you make, and I'd still find a way to put him in a class!"

I excused myself from the argument to explore her house. Hanging on the back wall, I noticed several crosses, ceramic masks, and a picture of Caucasian Jesus Christ.

"We have the same picture of Jesus at our house, too!"

Arguing.

"Right, Dad?"

More arguing.

"Dad?"

"What, Kenny?"

"Nothing... Never mind."

On the car ride back to my aunt and uncle's house, I sat beside Dad, astonished by how her appearance changed. Did I remember her correctly? I looked over at Dad as we turned a corner. "She looks different from how I remember her."

"Yeah." Dad sighed. "Sometimes grownups don't always make good decisions."

"Like what?"

"It's not important. Listen, son, I know I haven't been a perfect dad, but I want you to know I love you. Promise me you won't turn out like her when you're older."

"I promise."

"You don't want to get caught hanging around the wrong crowd, Kenny. It could ruin your life."

I'm a gymnast. Gymnasts don't end up in the wrong crowd.

I'll Be An Olympic Gymnast Someday

There were six weeks until the talent show, wherein I landed my backflip (on flat ground) for the first time. Mr. M concluded the morning with a math lesson when Jennette walked into the classroom with her mom. It was a Tuesday afternoon, almost lunchtime. I didn't understand nor enjoy the assignment, so I shoved it inside my desk, where several weeks of math homework lay crumpled.

"Hi, Mr. M!" Jennette's mom said, walking toward Mr. M's Desk. "I apologize my daughter is so late for class today; we just arrived back into town about an hour ago!"

Jennette skipped over to him ahead of her mom.

"What's this?" Mr. M asked, reaching for the picture frame in Jennette's hand.

Jennette beamed with pride. "It's from my gymnastics meet this weekend!"

"Gymnastics meet? Where?"

"It was an invitational!"

Jennette's mom repositioned her purse on her shoulder. "Yes! Mr. M, we flew to San Diego for the competition. Jennette will be competing at Westerns this year!"

"San Diego, eh? And what an impressive handstand on top of the high bar! I don't usually see students at this age compete at such a high level! How well did you compete this weekend?"

"I took second place in the All-Around!"

"Second place, huh? Very impressive." He lowered his glasses as if he were some philosopher. "You'll have to excuse me for a second. I would like to hear more about your weekend in SoCal."

He stood to address the class. "I need everyone to make a single file line at the door before I can release you for lunch!"

Screw going to lunch, I thought. I wanted to hear more, too. I tried to stay behind and eavesdrop on details about the gymnastics meet, although I didn't understand that the word 'meet' meant a competition.

"What's a gymnastics meeting?" I asked Jennette later at lunch.

"Don't worry about it, Kenny..."

"Well, I won't! Because I'm going to have a gymnastics meeting of my own!"

"Whatever you say," Jennette said while circling her finger around the side of her head, giggling with Megan.

Abel and his classmate, Jessica, rode their bicycles toward me in the distance. I waved at them from afar. "Abel! Jessica! Come here for a minute! I want to talk to you both!" They dropped their bikes in Abel's front yard and sprinted to me. "Listen up, guys! We are having a gymnastics meeting today!"

"What's a 'gymnastics meeting?'" Jessica asked.

"I'm not sure, but I think it's where you do gymnastics in front of the coach, and then they grade you or see how close you are to doing a trick."

Abel scratched his head. "But we don't have a coach."

"No problem, I can be your coach since I am better at gymnastics than you guys are." I swooped between them, put my arms around their shoulders, and marched into my yard. "Let's start with hand-stands, I guess."

"Okay."

"How many handstands have you done, Abel?"

He shrugged. "I don't know! I wasn't counting."

"Jessica?"

"Twelve, I think," she said, mid-handstand.

"Alright, well, that's enough. The handstands aren't perfect, but I can work with them. Let's take a look at your cartwheels!"

Jessica was a natural and could cartwheel all over the front yard. Abel, however, not so much. I tried helping him understand how to kick into a cartwheel without falling. I wanted him to imple-ment my corrections, but he couldn't. Jessica cartwheeled past us like a freight train for a split second, matching the speed of the cars that zipped down Bridgeport Avenue.

"She's athletic and efficient!" I said, hoping to inspire him to be better. "Kick your feet a little higher in this direction!"

I watched him kick up and crash. "No, you gotta place your hands here and kick over there. If you do it like that, you'll fall over again."

He made the same mistake.

"Abel!"

"What?" he asked, looking at me sincerely.

"We cannot progress this gymnastics meeting further if you can't figure out such a simple skill. You gotta get it together so we can move on to harder stuff."

He let out a bitter grunt. "Okay!"

After several minutes with numerous tips and suggestions, Abel still couldn't correctly land a cartwheel. He became increasingly frustrated at my demands, and I grew irritated at his failure. "Dude, you have to kick your feet above your head!"

Another failed attempt.

"Dude, even higher than that!"

When he fell again, I decided to change my coaching technique. "Oh, my God! Abel! You fucking idiot! Land on your feet!"

"I'm sorry!" he screamed, holding back his tears.

I decided to pull him aside. "Abel, I think it's time for your meeting. I've made my decision!" I said as we walked toward my porch. "As you can already tell, Jessica is way better than you at gymnastics so I'm ending your meeting here. I am also cutting you from all future meetings."

Abel stepped back and gave a furrowed look. "Fuck you, bitch!"

"Oh? Do you want me to tell your mom what you said?"

"I will never be your friend again, and you'll never come to our house ever again!" He taunted me while wiggling his body in weird directions as if trying to contort into another shape.

"You're gay, Abel. So go home!"

"You're gay, bitch!"

"Shut the fuck up, dude! You're immature and stupid. Go home before I tell your mom you cussed."

He stuck his tongue out at me and stormed away.

"Thank God he left," I looked at Jessica. "That was a nightmare!"

I looked back toward Abel, now yelling, trying to lift his bike to throw it across his front lawn with little success.

Jessica stood there watching him. "That boys got some serious anger issues."

I spent the next hour teaching her how to fall into a bridge position so she could eventually perform a back walkover. "I think it's time for your meeting. Let's go over to the bench on the side of the house," I motioned her to follow me. "So overall, I am impressed with your ability to master these skills. You were way better than Abel today! You practically blew him out of the water with your tumbling. A bit of coaching from me and I think you could be doing back handsprings in no time!"

Her eyes twinkled above her dirt-smudged cheeks. "Could you teach me tomorrow?"

"Maybe not tomorrow," I pulled a small dandelion out of her hair. "I have my own training to do, but someday yes!"

I wanted to be two or three skill levels ahead of Jessica. Jennette was already a better gymnast than me; I couldn't have my prodigies becoming better than me, too. After Jessica rode her bike home, I gathered all the blankets I could find and stacked them on each other, eight in total. I planned to spend the rest of the evening extrapolating the backhand spring I learned on Joel's trampoline and transferring it to flat ground. I wanted the skill in time for the talent show.

The next day before school, I stood outside Longfellow, waiting in line with the rest of my class for Mr. M to bring us inside. I walked over to Jennette. "I had a gymnastics meeting yesterday, and we practiced our skills!" I hopped backward into the grass. "Watch this!" Then, I put my arms in front of me to bend my body back until my hands touched the grass in a bridge pose.

"Wow," Jennette giggled sarcastically.

"Look what else I learned!" I said and jumped backward into a handspring. "Cool, huh?"

"Do you even know what a gymnastics meet is?"

"Nope. It doesn't matter to me, either. I still had one of my own! I'm officially a gymnast now!"

Jennette looked at me with disbelief, "well, it's called a 'meet,' not a 'meeting!'"

"So?"

"So you're not a real gymnast and you'll never be one!" The school bell rang; it was time for us to line up.

Near the end of elementary school, I told myself I was on my way to becoming an Olympic gymnast. Even though I had never stepped foot into a gymnastics facility, let alone any formal training in the sport. In the Spring of 2006, I sat on the floor in front of the whiteboard, where Mrs. S—my sixth-grade teacher—sat in her rocking chair. She passed around slips of paper to fill out. The assignment would become the quote for our yearbook.

The slip of paper said: *In 10 years I want to* _____

I considered education as a profession. Holding a red ink pen all day and bossing around children did sound fun. I even spent hours in my bedroom pretending to be a teacher while marking some of my unfinished assignments with the red ink pen I stole from Mrs. S's desk. My obsession with that sort of power ended because I hated school and seldom turned in homework.

"Everyone, Listen up!" Mrs. S announced. "I want you to think about the next ten years of your life. Where do you see yourself after graduating high school? Will you go to college? Trade school—"

"Does a family business count?" One kid yelled while raising his hand.

"It sure does! You can become anything you'd like. Some will be veterinarians, and others will be doctors or lawyers. I want you to think about what you want to be when you grow up, and write it on this slip of paper." She held the paper high for everyone to see. "When you are finished, please turn it into the basket at the front. I do not want any papers turned in that are crinkled, wrinkled, or dinkled!"

I began brainstorming. But I already knew I wanted to be an Olympic gymnast. I also knew Mrs. S wouldn't let me pick gymnastics as a career choice. But I wanted her and my classmates to know gymnastics was the career choice I had in mind and that someday, I'd be competing on the world's biggest stage. So I threw in some loaded terms like "study" and "college" to recruit her support:

IN TEN YEARS, I WANT TO GO TO COLLEGE FOR A FEW YEARS AND STUDY TO BECOME A BETTER GYMNAST SO THAT I CAN COMPETE IN THE OLYMPICS AND TRY TO WIN MEDALS.

Try to win medals, I wrote. After all, competing didn't guarantee I'd win an Olympic medal, but I'd qualify no matter what.

In the Fall, I began the seventh grade at Garry Middle School, a lifeless and prison-like structure with no personality. The building had few windows, with little to no color to the school's architecture: white walls, white lockers, no windows—the school's official slogan. One day in class, my Language Arts teacher, Mr. J, assigned the class a sheet of paper with thirty empty lines on the left-hand side of the page. "Alright, class. I want you to write your name on an empty line and pass the paper to the person to your right to sign the next empty line." At the end of the assignment, every kid in class had a page with twenty-five signatures. "This assignment was for fun, but someday, if one of you becomes famous, you'll each have their seventh-grade signature."

I thought it would be me once I made the Olympic team. My feelings and desire to accomplish an impressive feat in gymnastics intensified each day. I'd start my day riding the school bus and daydreaming about competing. Still, I saw no sign Mom or Dad planned to enroll in a gymnastics class anytime soon. Yet, I knew if I had any chance of making the Olympic team someday, I needed to be in a gym with a coach, and it needed to be now. I could feel my window of opportunity to begin training slip away. Would Lynn help pay for a class or two? One afternoon, I pleaded with Dad. "Would you put me in gymnastics if I can get Lynn to pay for gymnastics lessons?"

"I'll think about it, son," Dad said while zoned into the Seahawks' football game.

"You will?"

"Sure."

Lynn spent months trying to forge a relationship with me since my visit to her house the summer before. She never made me feel weird or stupid about wanting to be in gymnastics. Still, I continued to have hang-ups about her. I called her from Dad's cell phone to see if I could leverage her desire to be a mom to finance my aspirations. "Hi, it's Kenny! I'm calling from my dad's cell phone."

"Hi there, tweety! How are you doing?"

"I am well! I'm calling to say hi!"

"Is that so? You never give me a call."

"Yeah, I know. Sorry."

"What is it? What do you want?"

"I want to take gymnastics, but Dad won't pay for it."

"Put your dad on the phone for me, okay?"

I yelled out, "Dad! Lynn wants to speak with you."

Two days later, I stood with Dad in the lobby of Lilac City Gymnastics. I couldn't believe Lynn convinced Dad to bring me here. The pro shop along the wall displayed leotards, singlets, shorts, and branded T-shirts. I also saw a circular rack with more leotards in the middle of the lobby. The glass front desk showcased accessories all gymnasts need, like hair ties, high bar grips, and athletic tape—lots of athletic tape.

"Are you sure you want to do this?" Dad asked me.

"Uh, Duh!" I said, not thinking about how my response might have come across disrespectfully.

"Well, okay. If you want this, I'll support you where I can."

"Thanks, Dad."

I walked to the end of the lobby, where the main door led into the gym, while Dad filled out the paperwork.

"Dad, you have to see how awesome this place is!" I motioned him toward me. A man appeared at the door. "Hi! Are you, Kenny?"

"That's me!"

"I'm pleased to meet you! I'm Anders! The head boys' team coach!"

"Coach Anders! It's nice to meet you!" I acted sternly, trying to impersonate a soldier in training.

"Please, you can call me Anders!"

"Got it, sir!"

"Alright, you guys." Anders looked at a group of boys to my right. "Come on in! Kenny, just follow along with the rest of the boys."

I looked over at Dad, who stood before the door leading into the gym. "I'm going into practice now."

Dad returned a nod I had only seen once before. "Have a fun time, son!" His facial expression gave way to a similar look I saw the first time I walked to school without an adult escorting me. His smile appeared sad, yet his eyes beamed full of pride. I didn't know how to interpret his expression. Did he feel happy for me? Or did he feel disappointed in me? I couldn't tell.

On the spring floor, we sprinted corner to corner and jogged along the edges before another round of corner-to-corner sprints. I didn't feel tired because the floor made me feel superhuman. I looked at one of the boys beside me. "I'm used to doing flips on the grass. I bet you can get some serious height on this floor!"

"You get used to it, and it stops feeling bouncy," he replied.

"I don't believe that."

"You've only been here for like ten minutes. I'm here every day."

I enjoyed the line tumbling and the way Anders grabbed my legs and told me to point my toes. I loved sprinting as fast as possible to jump on the springboard to flip a front handspring over the vault table. Training in gymnastics gave me a rush of exhilaration unlike anything I'd ever felt.

"How am I doing?" I'd ask Anders every ten seconds. "Am I doing awesome?"

"You're excited to be here, aren't you? You're doing fine, Kenny. It's only your first day, so you don't have the level of technique I'm looking for. Time and practice will bring you to speed."

"Got it coach... I mean Anders, sir!" The only part of the practice I needed clarification on, perhaps even felt afraid of, was the high bar. "How does he swing around the bar in a handstand like that?"

"He's been swinging giants for a couple of months now. Skills like this don't develop overnight or at home on a trampoline." Anders studied the boy swinging giants on the high bar, "sometimes a coach is needed to develop certain skills."

At the end of the practice, Anders made everyone sit in the splits with our front legs higher on a mat. I didn't have my splits like everyone else. I wasn't even close. I told Anders I would catch up.

Anders pulled me aside after he dismissed the group. "How did you feel about today? Would you want to commit to the team if we offered you a spot?"

"Yes!"

"Alright, I'll contact your dad later this week to go over your commitment details."

"Thanks, Anders! I can't wait to join the team!"

Every day for two weeks, I waited in anticipation for the phone call from Anders because I desperately wanted to go back to the gym for my next practice.

"Did Lilac City call back today?" I asked Dad every day after school.

"Not today, son. I'm sure we'll hear back from them soon enough."

I wanted to be back in the gym. The gym was the only place that made me feel successful, even if I still lagged behind the other boys on the team. I couldn't focus at school because I could only think about my future in the sport. I wasted too many precious hours learning about subjects I didn't care about at Garry. Garry didn't enrich me in the same way Lilac City did. Some of my teachers at Garry made me feel stupid, lazy, or a combination of the two. My coaches at Lilac City made me feel capable and equipped to accept the challenge.

"It might feel scary, Kenny. But I believe in you, bud. You can do this!" I recalled what Anders said during my tryout.

Meanwhile, I made it difficult for teachers to engage me at Garry.

"Of course, you didn't turn in your homework... yet again." Most importantly, at Lilac City, I would make friends who shared a passion for the sport. It was the one place where I knew I'd fit in. Kids at the gym wouldn't call me weird or gay as kids at school did.

I arrived home from school one afternoon to Dad sitting on the porch with his shirt tucked into his work jeans and a pair of sunglasses covering his eyes.

"Hey, I've got news for you," he said.

"Yes?" I said, beaming.

"The, uh, gymnastics place called me back today."

I could scarcely contain my excitement. "When do I get to go back and train?"

"They didn't want you, Kenny. I'm sorry."

The Pretender

For several months after my rejection from Lilac City, I felt unmotivated, looked gaunt and unkempt, and faced a chaotic REM cycle. Mom and Dad, I think, could sense my defeatism—my dreams halted before a dam, yet my passion continued rising. I still wanted to compete in the Olympics. Gymnastics still captivated me, and now I stayed home, spending my free time in front of the family computer, thanks to my discovery of YouTube. YouTube had recently developed, allowing me to browse women's gymnastics videos. When Christmas morning arrived that year, Mom and Dad unexpectedly sent me on a scavenger hunt. I ran from the Christmas tree in the dining room to their bedroom, from their bedroom to the laundry room; from there, I ran outside to Mom's car to grab a note attached to the keys that read *check the shed.*

Dad unlocked the shed for me since I had trouble fiddling with the keyhole. I opened the door, and before me lay a large box with a blanket covering it.

My eyes grew wide. "Is that a—"

My aunt looked at my mom and dad. "Do you think he's going to scream like a little girl?"

I screamed like a little girl, "A trampoline! A trampoline! Thank you, thank you, thank you!"

I ran over to hug Mom and Dad. I interpreted the trampoline as their way of embracing my zest for gymnastics. They were coming around. Aside from making time to jump on my trampoline, YouTube became my latest obsession. I tuned into an elite eleven-year-old gymnast competing in a floor routine from 1993. She competed in the floor exercise using the same music as another gymnast who won the all-around title at the 1991 World Gymnastics Championships. I gasped. How could an eleven-year-old girl throw a full-twisting double backflip on the floor like that? How did she learn to overcome the fear without seriously getting injured? I would turn thirteen in the summer. Did my age disqualify me from training a full-twisting double backflip?

Mom walked through the front door toward the kitchen, holding several bags of groceries, while Dad sat on a stool tuning his electric guitar. I was sitting in front of the computer, watching the same gymnastics floor routine for the hundredth time that afternoon, imagining myself competing in the arena. I loved daydreaming, especially with the aid of YouTube.

"It sure would be wonderful if I had a son who could help bring groceries inside," Mom said on her way back out to the car.

"Go help your mom, Kenny," Dad said, not looking away from his guitar.

"One second!" I paused the video to sprint out to the car.

I returned from the car with two bags of groceries in each hand and saw Dad sitting at the computer scrutinizing the playlist. "Kenny, why do you keep obsessively watching girls' gymnastics?"

"It's only videos from the Olympics. Besides, look at how cool these flips are!" I started the video hoping to impress Dad with her full-twisting double backflip. "See? Mind you, she's only eleven!"

"This isn't normal, Kenny. Boys your age don't incessantly stare at videos of girls' gymnastics," he paused, "unless, of course, they're jacking off to it."

I suddenly felt nauseous. I wanted to sink into the floor. I stood in awkward silence.

Dad kept looking at me. "What? You do like girls, don't you?"

I pulled my long-sleeved shirt over my hands to hide them. "I mean, yeah. I guess."

"Are there any girls at school you like?"

My heart thumped out of my chest sporadically, and I broke eye contact. "Well... uh. I.." I hesitated. "There's this girl named Jennette. She does gymnastics."

"Uh-huh. I see. Why don't you play outside for a bit while mom cooks dinner. I'm going to make some noise with the guitar."

Did Dad believe my interest in gymnastics developed because of an attraction toward Jennette? Being attracted to her would have been expected. But it wasn't true. I didn't want to tell him *Zac Efron Naked* had been part of Google search history. I couldn't understand why the idea of growing into a man and publicly admitting a sexual interest at all made me feel dirty. I listened to how boys at school talked about female crushes, but I have never had one. Why did I not feel attracted to girls? Was there something wrong with me?

At Garry, I pretended I had thirty hours of gymnastics practice each week as an up-and-coming level 7 gymnast. But only with certain friends who might not be privy to the reality. I had no idea what I was talking about most of the time. I didn't even understand how the leveling system worked in the sport. I only understood what I heard from Jennette or gleaned from YouTube. But I didn't let my lack of knowledge deter me from building this image for myself, so I lied to everyone.

"Yeah. I'm about to be a level 7 gymnast!" I told a mutual friend who also took gymnastics.

She seemed excited for me. "Oh, cool! When do you get to compete in level 7?"

"In like two weeks. There's still a couple a few things I need to do first!"

"Like what?"

"I can't say. It's top secret."

Then, she seemed utterly confused by my response. "Oh. Okay."

If I couldn't officially be in gymnastics, I'd continue to immerse myself in the sport the second-best way—YouTube, the trampoline, and my imagination. Every day after school, I committed to memorizing the floor routines of several famous gymnasts from the 1990s. I could mentally visualize myself on the screen selling their performances. Since Mom and Dad weren't always home, I'd lock the front door so I could dance along and pretend to run into the tumbling passes by jumping around the living room as the video played on the monitor full screen.

Once, while dancing mid-routine, I heard the deadbolt unlocking. Mom and Dad walked in unexpectedly. They were supposed to be at the Northern Qwest Casino by now.

"What are you doing here?" Dad asked.

"Nothing!" I said, running to turn off the computer monitor. "Aren't you supposed to be at the casino by now?"

"We were. Your mom forgot her purse." He looked at me sitting next to the computer. "You're not... you know..." Dad said while making a jerking motion with his hand.

"Oh no, no, that's gross, Dad!"

"Why is the front door locked then?"

"Oh, that? I forgot to unlock it." I feigned laughter.

"You better not be prancing around like a little fairy princess again! All you do is spend hours in front of the computer watching videos of girls twirling around. Your behavior isn't normal! Walker and Abel don't act like this!" He said, throwing his hands up and slamming the front door on his way back to the car.

I escaped the cloud of shame by retreating to the backyard to continue my daydreaming where I left off, except this time, instead of the dance moves, I'd propel my body into sky-high backflips embodying elite-level gymnastics. YouTube mentally stimulated me while jumping on the trampoline burned the stored energy. I could merge the two aspects and pretend to be the coolest gymnast in the world; I could get lost in my imagination for hours, feeling like I was progressing. Still, I grew agitated with the glaring problem before me—I didn't have a coach or a facility to train at.

At the end of seventh grade, I decided to participate in the school talent show. To prepare for the audition, I opened LimeWire on the computer to search for any gymnastics floor music I could burn onto a blank CD and my MP3 Player. I wanted my performance to be as authentic as possible. While browsing the internet, I found a website that sold gymnastics floor music. All those songs sounded upbeat and fun. But I discovered a downside. The website charged fifty dollars per song. I enjoyed all the selections, but I couldn't afford them. So, LimeWire it was. I downloaded a couple of tunes and plugged a pair of headphones into my MP3 player that I attached to my shorts. I wanted it to stay secured as I jumped into pretend tumbling passes, choreographing my routine for the big day.

Bang! Bang! Bang! Dad pounded on my wall. "Quit prancing around like a sissy! You're not a girl!"

A tsunami of humiliation spilled over, and I paused for a moment. But I continued practicing my new floor routine, trying to stay lighter on my feet so I wouldn't get yelled at again. I flailed my arms elegantly around and pretended to jump into a leap before starting another pseudo-tumbling pass on the small space of my bedroom floor.

Bang! Bang! Bang! Dad pounded again. "I said quit jumping around!"

The sound of my door opening while jumping in the air mid-twirl caught me by surprise. I stopped, breathing heavily from the dancing. I looked at Dad, who cringed and began rubbing his forehead. I wanted to run away, but he kept his focus on me.

"Why Kenny? Why do you keep leaping around your room like a little fairy princess? You don't see Walker or Abel doing this shit, do you? Why can't you start acting like a normal teenage boy?"

Well, I'm not Walker or Abel, am I? I didn't yell back. I wanted to. I knew better than to talk back to Dad. He had no problem smacking me if I acted out of line. It wasn't uncommon for us to get into an argument that ended with him storming out of my bedroom only to burst the door open seconds later and ask, "What'd you say, boy?" I always felt like an asshole for being myself.

The day of the talent show, I sat in the chairs off to the side of the gym dressed in a pair of long-sleeved pajamas with assorted colored dinosaurs underneath shiny red Walmart-branded athletic shorts and the corresponding tank top. I thought I looked dressed for the part. There were still two acts ahead of me. I could feel the black hole growing in my stomach. Did I feel excited? Nervous? Where did the uncertainty originate? The students at Garry would easily remember my performance as the afternoon's headline. Nobody else, except for Jennette, could toss cool flips like me, but she didn't sign up to participate. The stage was all mine.

Several kids, primarily magicians and singers, partook in the show with me. Many singers in the show sang over the artist's voice. Their acts were more like a sing-along. I eagerly waited for the girl before me to finish her song because I knew I'd be next. "Wish me luck." I said to the girl who sang along to Avril Lavigne.

"Good luck! You've got this!"

My music selection from LimeWire was a ninety-second cut from the Pirates of the Caribbean. The music began playing loudly across the gym. I channeled the choreography I practiced in my bedroom. I pretended to mop the boat deck and even fearfully walked the plank before psyching the audience out with an inaudible "aye-aye captain!" Then, I ran into my first tumbling pass, a round-off backflip. I kept my tumbling passes on the quick beats because they gave me a rush of adrenaline. I performed what I imagined were elaborate moves with my arms and attempted a split jump, though I wasn't flexible enough to do the splits, followed by another round-off backflip. Then something happened; I forgot the choreography I had worked on in my bedroom. So, I swept the imaginary boat deck again, pretended to be a jolly pirate, and ran into several more backflips. That's why I auditioned: to show off my backflips. My body extended backward like a scorpion each time.

I searched my memory at the last minute and brought forward some of the dance moves I had seen on YouTube. I reached over the top of my head with my right arm like some caffeinated angler fish searching for rhythm. (Thanks, Kim Zmeskal!) I fell prone on the mat, kicking my feet and forearms while quickly looking left and right. (Thanks, Dominique Moceanu!) The dance moves neither fit the music nor the theme I choreographed at home. After running out of ideas, I stopped the routine mid-music and casually ran off the stage, waving to the audience as if I had planned it to end this way. The school erupted into thunderous cheers. I felt relieved. I hoped nobody noticed my mistake. Once I sat down, I felt offended that I wasn't the afternoon's final performance. Some eighth-graders dressed in sleeping bags with faces who danced around concluded the show.

Later, when I got home, I logged onto Myspace. There was an unread message from a kid I recognized from school. The message read something like this:

> *You looked fuckin gay out there. Ur a reel fag!*

I responded by calling him a cocksucker. He called me a faggot. I told him to shut the fuck up. He kept calling me a faggot. Then I got more messages from others echoing the same. So, I logged off Myspace.

The following week at school was pure damage control. "You guys! I did not wear dinosaur Pajamas! Gymnastics professionals designed my suit!"

An acquaintance at my lunch table said, "No, those were Dinosaur Pajamas. I could see them super well."

Even Joel wasn't coming to my defense, insisting in front of everyone else they were, in fact, dinosaur pajamas. "Dude... You wore them to my house for several sleepovers. Those were dinosaur Pajamas!"

"Oh my God! No, they fucking weren't!" I threw in the cuss words, hoping to convince them.

He smirked. "Yes, they were."

"Fuck you and get out of my life!" I said before stomping away.

It was too late. I couldn't take back the facts. I could only sit back and recoil at my school-wide ridicule. This incident was my fault. I should have never entered the show. Maybe I could laugh it off with everyone else. Perhaps I could spin my talent show routine as a comedy act? Instead, rumors about my sexuality began circulating, and classmates asked me the same question:

"Are you gay?"

I should have started liking girls by now, but I didn't. I liked boys instead. But I feared the consequences of letting anyone know the truth about me. I felt horrible enough getting bullied for suspicions. I could only imagine what it would be like if everyone discovered my secret. I feared Mom and Dad would be furious if they found out. It was true, though. I was turning out gay, which meant I'd go to Hell, and I didn't want to go there. There had to be something I could do to reverse this course of my life.

The author. Summer 2007.

The Scariest Movie of all Time

I spent my early teen years asking God for forgiveness so He wouldn't send me to Hell after I died. The belief system Mom and Dad raised me in gave me night sweats and knots in my stomach. We were a Christian family, although we rarely, if ever, attended church. There is room for debate about how I perceived God and Jesus in my youth. Perhaps I believed a blended mix of the two backgrounds in which Mom and Dad grew up—Jehovah's Witness on Mom's side and Baptist or Presbyterian on Dad's. But I understood all too well the implication of my parents' faith—don't do bad things, or you'll go to Hell. Mom and Dad used the threat of Hell as a behavior modification technique. It would thrive vibrantly like a parasite in my psyche, following me everywhere I went. If I misbehaved or acted out, they'd remind me of my potential destination by pointing to the ground while making a worried face. The problem for me: I was a proficient delinquent. I got poor marks in school; I talked back, lied fluently, and was an unskilled kleptomaniac.

My late grandmother's hardcover copy of the King James Bible had a permanent residence on the coffee table in our living room. As a family, we always prayed together before big family meals like Thanksgiving and Christmas. Dad made sure to be more disciplined in his faith; he prayed before every meal. Inside our house, I remember several crosses, depictions of angels, and a painting of Jesus hanging on the wall to remind us, well, me, that He had the authority to condemn. I didn't have a concrete understanding of the Christian faith, only what I had learned second-hand from my cousin Dakota or the occasional preaching from a televangelist. As I grew older and my sexual preferences became more apparent, the Christian way of living felt more and more unobtainable. Why would I go to Hell for being attracted to men? I didn't choose to be gay. The gospel message Christians seemed to peddle forth created unnecessary perturbations about my life. Still, I wanted to be baptized, to check all the boxes—just in case.

Mom and Dad planted the early seeds of indoctrination, and a little further along the timeline, feelings of inadequacy and eternal damnation sprouted at the top of this exotic beast of a tree. The not-so-basics were grafted into me like a dental implant, grounding me in skewed beliefs about God, faith, and the afterlife. In high school, I began confronting my same-gender attraction as something that needed purging. But I also wanted to indulge in every aspect of it. If being gay disqualified me from Heaven, that felt unfair. What about all the other misdeeds I had already done in life? Judging whether God wrote me on His naughty or nice list felt difficult. It had something to do with the purity of childhood and the exact point wherein a person becomes accountable for their actions. Where should I have drawn the line? What if I died young? Worse, what if—

I was eleven or twelve when my curiosity led to defiance. Oh, there's nothing more gratifying than being young and defiant. I had a sleepover with Walker and Abel at their house when Susan called out to us from her bedroom. "Hey, boys! Come here for a second." Walker and I skipped over to her door. She sat up in her bed, filing her nails. "Don't disturb Chelsea and her friends in their room tonight. They're going to be watching a scary movie!"

"But what if we want to watch it, too?" Walker asked, holding the VHS sleeve.

"No! You boys are way too young to watch that."

"No, I'm not!" I said. "I'm almost a teenager! I can watch anything I want to!" And I did. I watched plenty of horror films, from *Child's Play* to the Rob Zombie film *House of 1000 Corpses*. I wasn't afraid of anything.

"Yeah, right. Go ask your mom right now and see what she says," she dared. We accepted and gladly sprinted across the gravel and patches of dead grass leading to my house.

"Mom! Mom! Mom!" I shouted, bursting the door open.

"What honey?" she asked, sitting in her recliner watching T.V.

"Can we watch *The Exorcist*? Susan thinks we're too young."

"No, you may not!"

"But, Mom, it's supposed to be scary."

"I don't care, Kenny! You're not watching that film! It's evil and based on a true story!"

"Yeah! So? *The Amityville Horror* is based on a true story, but you let me watch that!"

"My answer is still no."

"Please!"

"Your mother said no, Kenny," Dad said, sitting in the recliner beside Mom, "now run, fly, be free!"

Feeling dejected, we decided to go back and build a fort in Walker's bedroom using sheets and his bunk bed. I grabbed the VHS sleeve on my way into his bedroom. I looked down at the cover that read something to the effect of *The Title of the Movie, followed by a blurb about how terrifying it is in a version previously unseen,* in bold letters across the front.

"*The Exorcist,*" I said softly. "Doesn't even look scary to me." I tucked my end of the sheet underneath the top bunk's mattress. I wanted to know the reason for such confidence. It's bold for a director to claim their movie is the scariest. On the backside, a ghostly bright light shone from a top-floor window, illuminating a shadowy figure holding a briefcase. Perhaps a detective? What did 'exorcist' mean anyway? Next, a red picture of a little girl glaring in the top left corner of the sleeve and more pompous writing about the movie's supposed terror. "It can't be any scarier than Poltergeist. Does it even look scary to you?"

"No, it doesn't," Walker said.

I set the cover aside. "We have to watch it! Let's sneak it over to my house later! We have a VCR and a T.V. downstairs we can use!"

Walker nodded. "I'm down!"

"And me too!" Abel added.

A few days later, we did. I popped the VHS into the VCR. Walker had snuck the film over by switching VHS sleeves with That Darn Cat, so we made it a point to periodically yell out, "That darn cat!" while laughing obnoxiously. Did our acting seem convincing enough? No, but nobody investigated what we were doing, either.

"This is so boring," I said, "there's nothing scary about this at all." We were nearing the midpoint of the film. It progressed slowly.

Walker kept his gaze on the T.V. "Yeah, I don't get it either."

Suddenly, we heard a crash and some scuffling. Then, a deep voice rumbled in the background as the mother in the movie blazed the staircase to her daughter's bedroom. The daughter in the film screamed while the deep voice coming from within her called her *a very mean name*. The daughter continued bellowing horrific screams while the sound of breaking glass filled the room, and vinyl records crashed into the window. The entity controlling her began shoving a bloodied metal religious object into *her private part*, basically commanding her to get fucked by a historical figure from the Bible. Her face—covered in red corn syrup—looked of sheer evil.

The scene was so intense I shrieked, "Okay, That's enough!" I rushed over to turn the film off. We sat silently for several minutes.

Walker put his hand over his heart. "My heart is racing so fast!"

I agreed, "Yeah, I did not expect this at all!"

Abel had run out of the bedroom mid-scene.

I couldn't sleep that night. Or the next night. Or the next night after that. Every night, I'd keep still, paralyzed with fear. The sound of my heartbeat was enough to send me into a panic. Sometimes, I could hear loud breathing that wasn't my own. I'd get out of bed and sprint into the pitch-black dining room upstairs. It took several hours to come to my senses and fall asleep. The only way to get me through the panic was by developing a mantra: *I've got God and Jesus in my heart.*

The next afternoon, I walked through the kitchen door and saw Mom grating boiled eggs into freshly cooked macaroni noodles. My cat, Z.Z., rubbed his head against me, shedding black fur onto my leg.

"Whatcha cooking?"

"Macaroni salad. Your dad is going to light the barbecue."

"Oh, cool. I have a question."

"What's up, hun?"

"*The Exorcist,* It's not a true story. Right? It's all Hollywood?"

"It's a true story. That's why you won't be bringing that Devil crap into my house!"

"Ohhh. Okay," I said, "Because I didn't watch it."

"You better not have! We've only got room for God and Jesus in this house!" She said, turning to grab a giant spoon to mix the salad, "can you get the mustard, mayonnaise, and pickles from the fridge?"

I am so fucked.

I didn't know what to do or who to talk to. I panicked for several weeks over the possibility of becoming possessed by some powerful demon. I'd have to face my fears alone. As time passed, however, demonic possession became my secret obsession. I Googled anything I could find and discovered ways to throw the topic into conversation with friends at school.

"Did you know Linda Blair, the little girl who played the main character in the movie *The Exorcist,* was possessed before in real life!" I said, lying to one of my classmates.

"Who is Linda Blair? What is that?"

"Don't tell me you haven't seen *The Exorcist!* It's only like the scariest movie of all time! But I'm a stronger person now, having watched it already!"

"Oh... okay."

Other times, I mocked friends for not knowing what I was talking about, "Wait. You haven't seen *The Exorcist*? How embarrassing!"

None of my peers at school seemed even remotely interested in my topic of interest. While they were studying the historical person they planned to represent at the upcoming sixth-grade wax museum presentation, I researched exorcisms and their effect on modern society (not really, but you get the picture). I even pretended to be possessed to prepare for my presentation.

I walked over to Mrs. S's table, "Can I portray Linda Blair as the main character from *The Exorcist* at the Wax Museum on Friday?"

"What?" She asked, looking slightly concerned. "Why don't you pick a strong male to present?"

"Okay... What about Max Von Sydow? He played the Priest in the same film!"

"Oh, good gravy... No! You pick someone else and maybe another topic while we're at it. You know, something appropriate for school? How about Dr. Suess?" Mrs. S said, smiling.

"Fine," I rolled my eyes while walking away. "I'll be Dr. Suess."

How could I face my fears if I couldn't act them out at the children's wax museum? During the daytime, everything felt fine. But once nighttime rolled around, a black hole that made me feel nauseous and full of dread filled my stomach. Was this feeling the genesis of demonic possession? Was I moments away from involuntarily showing the classic signs, like in the movie? I wanted to hug Z.Z. He always comforted me if I could locate him before bed.

On a cool Sunday morning, Walker and I rode our bikes around the neighborhood.

"I need to find a priest!" I yelled out.

He trailed behind me. We rode our bikes along Euclid Street, a few miles past Gonzaga Prep High School. At the end of Euclid, we turned right on Market Street toward the community college and rode along the river until I noticed the church I wanted to enter. "There's our target!" I yelled behind me, speeding ahead. I hopped off my bike and leaned against the rails leading to the church's front doors. Many attendees were sitting and worshiping Jesus in song. After the service ended, I approached the pastor of the congregation.

"Have you ever performed an exorcism?"

"Uh," He chuckled, "that's an interesting question. But no, I've never performed an exorcism."

"I need to know if I have a real chance of becoming demonically possessed by a demon or even the devil himself!"

"Where is this coming from?"

"I watched *The Exorcist*... You know the 1973 classic with Linda Blair and Ellen Burstyn?"

He raised an eyebrow. "That's a bit before my time, but I'll take your word for it! Are you afraid of it happening to you?"

"Yes! I wouldn't have come here if it weren't the case!"

"Well... that's all Hollywood. The real question is... Do you, Kenny, have God and Jesus in your heart?"

"Yeah, I guess."

"I invite you to accept Jesus into your heart. All you need to do is read this prayer in faith," the pastor handed me a slip of paper. "And you'll be safe from evil."

"Thanks man!"

"No problem, and come back again soon!"

"I will, thank you!"

I didn't return.

Around high school, I began taking a serious approach to faith. A few weeks before Halloween, Dad drove us to the Shadle Park Walmart to purchase decorations for the house. I help up a tiny skeleton. "When can I get baptized?"

"Soon, son," Dad turned around. "I was thinking about taking your mom and me to get baptized again, too."

I grabbed a pack of spiderwebs and threw them into the basket. "Why do we need to be baptized anyway?"

"Well, son. It's how God washes your sins away," He said, holding a fall-scented candle. "Do you think your momma would like this?"

"I like the smell! "I said, "so, baptism is like how you get into heaven?"

"Well, you can't go to heaven with sin, so I'd say so."

"When do you think we could do this? I would like to get baptized."

Dad stopped the cart to throw in some orange and purple lights. "Soon. We can plan a family dunking session sometime."

We were walking toward the checkout when I blurted out, "Can you get me one of these Bibles?"

He looked at me and the Bibles and nodded in approval. Perhaps a personal bible would offer me protection against Satanic forces. For all I know, Dad believed it would lead me onto the correct path. I'd kept the paper prayer the preacher gave me for several years. I could store it in my Bible when I slept at night. I wanted the extra protection because what if I did become possessed by the devil?

August, 2008. I had a negative view of John R. Rogers High School the summer before my freshman year. Most of the information I gleaned about the school came second-hand from my brother and sister and their friends, who had all been students there in the early 2000s. Was I about to be thrown into the lion's den? How I acted, they told me, wouldn't fly at Rogers—I'd get pummeled every day if I didn't man up. Rogers was collectively known as The Bad Kid School. I assumed I had plenty to fear on my first day. My experience, however, did not square away with what I had heard. Students and teachers worked overtime to show the community what it meant to be a Rogers Pirate. I attended a school that put in the work to rise above how everyone else viewed us.

The negative perception, however, was challenging to shed, given the media's stereotypical portrayal of Hillyard—and, more specifically—Rogers. Did a shooting occur in Hillyard? It happened to be near Rogers. Swat standoff in North Spokane? It was also conveniently located near Rogers. Did somebody get arrested in connection to a dead body? It seemed too juicy not to include Rogers. Yes, bad things happened in Hillyard, but the news always saw it fit to paint Rogers negatively. The assumption that came to mind was that Rogers prepared future inmates instead of productive members of society. How did Rogers, or its student population, connect to all these mishaps? It didn't. Rogers stood as the recognizable monolith in a low-income part of town—the media's proverbial punching bag. Even to this day, it seems outsiders recognize Rogers as a place synonymous with violence and crime. But it's not really like that. There's a lot of heart and soul there. To outsiders, Rogers High School remains the Bad Kid School. But to us, we were the Pirates. *Familia Sumas.*

As a freshman, I felt optimistic for a brighter future. I had flunked my way through school to this point. I looked to the start of high school as an excellent time to reinvent myself. I would study diligently and do my homework, I said. I even created goals and benchmarks and tried to look at my future seriously after high school. Whatever I did in life, I hoped to become financially stable. During orientation, one of my teachers presented a video about famous failures. The video highlighted people like Michael Jordan, who got cut from his high school basketball team, or Thomas Edison, whose teacher said he was "too stupid to learn anything." I reflected on my ambitions and viewed the roadblocks in my journey thus far as part of the bigger picture of success. After I became an Olympian, it would all be worth the pain and frustration. I felt so sure of my success that I even signed the yearbooks of some of my former teachers to the effect of: "Look for me in the 2012 Olympics!"

I had only one goal in mind at Rogers—to join the gymnastics team, and it felt all-consuming. I did join but could only train because the Greater Spokane League (GSL) only offered gymnastics to girls. The Title IX rules barred me from competing. Title IX ensures equal opportunities for girls to participate in athletics. It had become clear I wasn't going anywhere with the sport. What hurt worse was standing by watching the GSL make accommodations for girls to wrestle. So *much for Title IX,* I thought.

In lieu of gymnastics, I switched gears my sophomore year and joined the cross country team. After all, long-distance running seemed pretty straightforward. My expectations were minimal; I had no idea what I signed up for. To prepare for my first race, I bought two packs of Starbursts. The race was against Mead and North Central High School.

"You sure you wanna eat all that candy before the race?" One of my teammates asked me as we began our warmup.

I popped two in my mouth and started chewing. "Duh. It'll give me energy."

"I don't think it will."

"Relax, dude. It's only a little candy. I eat it all the time. I'll be fine."

"Okay. If you say so."

North Central High School had been the 2008 Nike National Champions the year before. Waiting for the race to start, I stood at the start line, utterly oblivious. After the gunshot, the group of runners began sprinting reasonably quickly. I vaguely remembered hearing from my coach, Miss. Driscoll, that I needed a solid start to the race. Afterward, runners could settle into their pace. Immediately, my stomach hurt, I couldn't breathe, and I wanted to vomit the chocolate milk and cheeseburger I had eaten for lunch. Not to mention all the starbursts I gobbled minutes before.

In what felt like an all-out sprint, the pack leaders showed no signs of slowing. And they didn't. After running a mile and a half, I had to stop and walk to catch my breath when suddenly it hit me: the top six runners from both schools were passing me. I finished the 5k, barely. From then on, I wanted to quit because I got lightheaded and panicky at the prospect of racing against North Central and Mead again. I didn't stack up. I continued running, however, because my closest friend, Anna Truong, trained with the boy's team, and I enjoyed hanging out with her at practice. The workouts were grueling, and I made a lazy effort. I hardly trained to my full potential. Cross Country and Track weren't my true calling; they were only temporary distractions. Moreover, I flopped my goals of academically reinventing myself in the first semester by earning Ds and Fs.

"Athletes cannot participate in competition until all grades are passing!" Miss. Driscoll often reminded our group before every competition. "High school alone is difficult enough; I'm always here for additional tutoring if anyone needs it," she'd add to reassure stragglers like me that it was possible to juggle academics and extracurriculars. As a result, I sometimes didn't get to race due to failing grades. But I felt at ease with it. Again, running cross country distracted me. Enduring these practices felt better than being at home.

The evenings at home were spent with Dad, drinking Hurricane High Gravities, rattling off outlandish conspiracy theories—FEMA camps and aliens inhabiting the Hollywood Elite. Most often, Dad spoke long monologues in whispered tones. What he said often didn't make sense, so hearers were left confused, listening as his conversation wafted around the room without a clear destination. Dad wasn't always like this, though. I remember him as busy and persevering. I recall Dad leaving the house at 6:00 a.m. before sunrise in below-freezing temperatures. Winters in the Pacific Northwest can be harsh, but Dad faithfully showed up to his job at the Spokane Rain Gutter, Inc. to climb roofs and replace, well, gutter helmets. His entire personality changed seemingly overnight in the winter of 2008. I am only left to wonder whether the economic recession had anything to do with it.

Anna Truong and the author at Lake Coeur d'Alene. Summer 2010.

Seeking God

Six months before graduation, I sat in bed writing the essay for my culminating senior project. While revising the rough draft, Dad barged into my bedroom, lit a cigarette, and mumbled off some slurred plea, "It's getting close, son!"

"Dad!" I barked. "Put out your cigarette! You cannot smoke in the house!"

"I can do what I want; it's my house now. It's going to happen soon! Get prepared."

"Get prepared for what? What are you talking about?"

"You'll know soon enough, son. You'll see," he took a drag and blew the smoke into the hallway outside my bedroom. "You need to get baptized."

He leaned into my doorway, softening his voice, "I'm sorry I never took you as a kid. I had meant to, but we got busy with life. We never had time for church."

"Alright, Dad, we can check one out together this Sunday!"

"No, Kenny. You'll have to go on your own. Your old man can't come along. You wouldn't want to see what happens next."

Dad was tugging at my naivety. I still hadn't been baptized, so I finally sought a church. One frigid Sunday morning, I rode my bike to the familiar church building near the community college. It had been six years since I last visited this building, and I still thought about the pastor who prayed with me. Perhaps he still ministered. I felt disappointed to discover the original church had vacated the premises, and, in its stead, a new congregation under a different name took residence.

I arrived ten minutes before the service began. I could feel my heart rate picking up as I dawdled toward the building. The pounding in my chest intensified with each step I took. From a distance, I watched curiously as members idly congregated in small circles, sipping coffee and snacking on complimentary doughnuts in the foyer. I told myself to keep going. I could do this. Standing by the doors were two greeters cheerfully welcoming everyone who came through.

"Hi, welcome in!" They said with merriment.

"Thanks," I responded coolly.

After entering, I froze in the foyer, faking a smile despite wanting zero social interaction with anybody. I scampered into the sanctuary, hoping to find a seat in the back, away from everybody. On the back wall, a projector revealed a timer. I watched as the timer counted in reverse from 03:56:47 to 03:55:34 above the stage. Everything happened in slow motion. I needed to make it through the service. Afterward, I could leave as quickly as I arrived. I sat in an empty chair, rested my hands on my lap, then inhaled sharply. Suddenly, a man appeared in the distance, full speed in my direction. "What's up, man? Welcome to church! I'm Asher!" He said with a slight Hebrew accent, extending his hand.

I obliged, and he gripped my shoulder and pulled me into a side hug he had not prepared me for.

"I'm Kenny. It's nice to meet you," I said mid-hug, awkwardly patting him on the shoulder.

I took note of Asher's eclectic and forthcoming personality. I couldn't help but gush over how tall and muscular he was. He resembled a Mormon Missionary, except rugged, with a neatly trimmed black beard beautifully contrasting his fresh fade. His arms fit snugly into his long-sleeved button-up, biceps protruding as if they might rip the sleeves at any moment; his slacks also tight around the buttocks. He hovered over me at six feet five inches like some California redwood.

"So, what brings you to church today?"

"Uh," I paused. "I need to be baptized. I don't want to go to Hell for not being baptized, you know?"

"Hold that thought, Kenny. I'll be right back."

Asher paved his way across the sanctuary, members parting for him like the Red Sea. He gave a couple of quick hugs, exchanging brief pleasantries, and then disappeared from my sight in the crowd. I awkwardly sat on the chair for several minutes, awaiting his return.

"Kenny!" Asher called out from across the way.

"This is Parker," he said, clasping his hands together as if praying, then pointed all four fingers at Parker. The gesture made me feel like he was hiding a secret. "Parker is training to be a ministry leader in Post Falls. He'd like us all to get together sometime for a bible study before we can baptize you."

"If that's okay with you." Parker jumped in.

"Bible study? Oh no. I'm here to get baptized."

Parker drew a look of confusion. "Kenny, we'd love to baptize you, but we must go over these bible studies with you. Baptism is a commitment, and we want to ensure you are ready before committing to our church."

"Oh, okay."

The timer on the screen had expired with six flashing zeros and an announcement from the evangelist standing at a podium urging everybody to find their seats. Asher asked if I wanted to sit with him as he strutted ahead, waving for me to follow him.

"This is where all of the cool people sit!" One of the girls sitting in the second row said.

"Oh awesome!" I sat in one of two empty seats.

"Save this spot for me!" Asher followed Parker and a few others to a small set of stairs connected to the main stage.

"Good morning, Church! Open your song books to song four sixty-two; 'I Know That My Redeemer Lives.'"

Everybody in the sanctuary stood together. It seemed odd but not unexpected. The few times I attended a service, I watched members sit to worship while maybe one or two outlier members stood to sing their praises to God. The pressure from the environment to join in the singing made me uncomfortable. I stood as the odd one out, not singing, which made me uneasy. It came across as a design to promote unity but also conformity. I fixed my eyes on Asher, singing and snapping his fingers with three others. Soon, snaps turned to claps, and everybody moved to the music. The church had the collective voice of an angel bouncing off the walls. A feeling of euphoria briefly painted me onto the canvas before snapping back to reality. I must have been the only introvert among a hundred extroverts, mouthing words and pretending to sing. Looking around and smiling was my only way of disguising the discomfort.

The worship wrapped. Asher returned. A provocative, joyful, numb feeling folded me inward when he sat down. How was it possible to be so goddamned sexy? He wore a cologne that made me giddy around him.

"I'm glad you decided to attend our church, Kenny!" He whispered.

I felt glad, too.

The lead evangelist preached a message about hope or love, or maybe he spoke about faith. I don't remember. The only thing I could focus on was how it felt to sit in the presence of Asher. I was instantly attracted to him the moment he first caught my eye. But I quickly learned of his engagement to the girl who sat to his right, the self-proclaimed leader of the Cool Kids Club—she introduced herself as Mirabel. Where did this congregation stand on gay marriage? I had only told a few people about my sexuality. I felt too afraid of what would come after. Rejection? More bullying at school? It all sounded rough. I hoped they would be supportive, but I didn't hold my breath on the matter because all Christianity had told me was how immoral homosexuality was.

"What day works for you to study the bible with us?" Parker asked as everyone mingled outside the building after service.

"I am usually free around six pm most days."

"How does this Friday at 6:30 work for you? The Starbucks on Market Street is still open then; can we meet there?"

"I can make 6:30 work!" Asher said.

"Alright, I guess I'll see you all Friday," I said.

Asher gave me a business card with his name and number: Asher *Yosef, Campus Ministry Intern, Post Falls International Church of Christ.*

I took the card. "Idaho?"

"It's only a half hour away from here. You're welcome to join Parker and I for house church tonight. It starts at 6:00 p.m."

"Oh, I don't have a car."

"No problem," he nudged me. "I can pick you up and drop you off later," he said, winking at me.

Asher was handsome and friendly and seemed eager to get to know me. I didn't want to pass up an opportunity to be with him, so I attended church that night in Post Falls.

The Bible study felt like an interrogation. I assumed the get-together would be another run-of-the-mill conversation to build camaraderie among already like-minded individuals. But this time, I wasn't sure.

Parker and Asher pulled out their marked-up lay-flat New International Versions of the Holy Bible and sat them neatly on the table.

"We both agree you look like you are seeking God, so we will be skipping that study in the series. It would be pointless to go over what we have determined to be true," Parker said, glancing at Asher and back to me.

What did he mean?

"What do you mean by seeking God?" I asked

"Good question. We want believers who will be truly committed to the teachings of Jesus Christ. The Seeking God study helps us to weed out false believers from the true believers."

"Oh, okay."

"Let's open our bibles to 2 Timothy 3:16-17. Asher, will you read the passage for us?"

"My pleasure!" He said. "'All scripture is God-breathed and is useful for teaching, rebuking, correcting, and training in righteousness, so that the servant of God may be thoroughly equipped for every good work.'"

"What do you think about this passage, Kenny?" Asher asked.

"I mean it makes sense."

"What makes sense?"

"The bible is for teaching Christians."

Parker pointed at the scripture. "The verse here says, 'all scripture is breathed out by God.' Meaning God has divinely inspired every word you read in the Bible."

He closed his Bible. "Do you know what Biblical Discipleship is, Kenny?"

"I've heard of the word before, I think."

"But do you know what it means? Sometimes churches might carry a different definition of the term and we want to make sure you have a clear, biblical definition."

"I guess I can't say I do."

Asher and Parker appeared well-rehearsed and thoroughly researched on the topic of Christianity. I was astounded by how they could effortlessly navigate each book in the Bible.

Parker and Asher began hosting me for one-on-one Bible studies before church. Sometimes, we'd meet in Parker's living room before church. Other times, Asher would drive us to meet at a Starbucks in Coeur d'Alene. I concluded these 'studies' were a subtle explanation of why I was not a faithful Christian. They made it seem like anyone not part of their church wasn't Christian. Still, it made sense. These guys wanted to ensure I made it to Heaven.

At Starbucks, I took a seat next to Asher. "So, you mean to say the churches I attended as a kid weren't helping me in my walk with God?"

"I mean, yes and no," Asher said. "They only promote the idea of Godly values. They might have a form of Godliness but will deny its power. The truth is, Kenny, if you want to be a real Christian, you have to become a sold-out disciple of Jesus."

"When can I get baptized?"

"Well, how is your faith?" Parker asked

"What do you mean by that?"

"Come on man. We've been studying the Bible for how long now?" He asked sharply. "You don't know what I mean?"

"I'm sorry. I don't."

Parker sighed. "Are you struggling with sin? Impurity or temptations? If you want to be saved, Kenny, you need to prove to us you're willing to work on your inner self to become sold-out before we can dunk you. You need to repent of all your sins."

"So, my faith is hindered by the sins I commit?"

"Lying, stealing, covetousness, licentiousness, gluttony, sexual immorality," Parker paused. "Homosexuality"—as if to say he knew my secret.

Asher nodded in support.

"Uh huh," I said.

"Look." Parker said, grabbing a piece of paper his wife handed him, who sat at another table. "This paper has God on one side of a brick wall and you on the opposite side. Your sin is like this brick wall; it separates you from the love of Christ. If you continue to live in sin, the higher the brick wall becomes; the further you become alienated from Christ. Repentance is the only way to demolish the wall."

Parker flipped the pages of his Bible to a passage from the Book of James. He put his finger on the page and began to read aloud, "'Therefore confess your sins to each another and pray for each another so that you may be healed.'"

Asher took a sip from his coffee. "Would you consider yourself a homosexual?"

My response impulsively slipped out, "I guess."

I wanted to take it back and tell them I wasn't gay; I was straight. But it wasn't true. I had disclosed my sexuality to a handful of girlfriends from school. But that was it. I wasn't ready to come publicly out of the closet yet.

"Have you ever acted out on your sin?"

"No, I haven't."

"You know," Parker chose his words, "You will need to conform to the teachings of the Bible to get right with God."

"I know. So when can I get baptized?"

"I don't think you're ready for that, Kenny."

"Baptism is the starting point of a persons salvation, right?"

"Yes."

"So then can I get baptized and then we continue studying?"

"It doesn't work like that, Kenny. You first need to become a disciple, and as I've already said, I don't think you're ready."

What if I died before I could meet their standard and get baptized? Were they withholding God's salvation from me? I found no solace in the direction the Bible Studies traversed. I didn't want to continue. I couldn't fathom the idea of suppressing my sexuality every day for God to consider me righteous. But I felt like I had no choice if I wanted Jesus to save me. I reluctantly continued the Bible studies, hoping my baptism would take place sooner than later. I told myself I could always leave the church if it became too much. Once I got baptized, I would at least have a safety net.

I began forging relationships in the church left and right. Everybody wanted to get to know me. I felt loved, and everyone encouraged me in my walk with God. The latest sister in the faith, a student at Northern Idaho College, had been baptized in Parker's backyard right after church concluded the previous week, so I felt enthusiastic and ready to commit to becoming a church member. However, every study proved exceedingly invasive, each uncovering another sin to eradicate, attached to another rule to follow. At Starbucks, I watched as baristas called out orders and customers hurried out.

I have a Venti Iced Soy Vanilla Latte for Suzanne!

"There's a lot of rules to follow in the faith, and to be frank, I am not confident I can follow through with all of them. Can't I commit to three or four rules and call it a day?"

"No!" Parker giggled. "You gotta be committed to Jesus. There is only one option to be saved. You cannot be a sinner and be a saved Christian. Jesus is the only way!"

How could anyone follow through with all these demands of discipleship? All my interrogations leaned toward my disposition.

"Not even blowjobs are allowed if you want to remain faithful to God," Asher said, scooping a handful of walnuts into his mouth.

Parker piggybacked while Asher chewed. "Sexual purity is the standard whether someone is gay or straight, Kenny. Two active homosexuals are as impure as an unmarried straight couple acting out sexually."

"So why can't two men be married?"

"Because, Kenny, the Bible is clear on the matter. Homosexuality is a sin!"

Asher had printed out several scriptures and slid them across the table. "Mark these in your Bible. You'll want to keep these handy in times of struggle."

"I was born a certain way, and God wants me to be the opposite? Make it make sense!"

"You were not born this way, Kenny! Stop your nonsense!" Parker rebutted.

"Look," I said, "my cousin has a degree in theology. Him and his wife say it's not a big deal."

"Oh, okay!" Parker shrugged. "Let me get this straight. You want to listen to your cousin who is trying to lead you astray? Let's open our bibles, shall we? Here is what your cousin is saying and here is what the Bible says. Who are you going to trust more? Your cousin? Or the Bible? Your feelings? Or the Bible?"

I couldn't digest the harsh commands.

"The Bible... I guess."

"Discipleship isn't easy, Kenny," he pointed to his Bible. "Broad is the road that leads to destruction. Narrow is the gate, and few find it."

I wanted to believe my cousin, but I knew these guys would only baptize me if I agreed with their teaching. I wanted my feelings to be valid, but baptism was my end goal; I wanted to go to Heaven.

I forged ahead. "Do I need to become straight for God to save me?"

Asher looked at me. "It's not about that. Heterosexuality isn't the opposite of homosexuality. The opposite of homosexuality is holiness. God wants you to be holy."

I felt depleted after every meeting. I had no option but to abandon homosexuality if I were to make it to Heaven. I believed my sexuality was the only issue stopping me from a genuine relationship with Jesus. The guys steered the conversation in a new direction, selling me several takes on the benefit of abandoning it. They explained that it provided a false comfort and a false identity. They said Satan sold homosexuality as a lie to pull people away from Christ.

I couldn't stomach the dilemma; I wanted to puke. "Why would God put me on earth and not be concerned with my happiness?" I pleaded with Parker. I wanted him and Asher to change their minds on the issue and make an exception for me.

Parker closed his Bible. "God sent his son to die on the cross. Afterward, his initial followers, were barbarically murdered for their faith in Jesus. Do you think God is concerned with your happiness here on earth? He wants your soul, not your happiness. Kenny, you need a serious reality check! It's time to decide whether you want to be saved or not. Jesus is knocking; it's your decision to open the door for Him."

"What comes next?" I asked impatiently. I wanted to hurry and get all of this over with. I tried to rip the bandaid off—so to speak—and assuage concerns so they'd feel ready to baptize me. After service on Sunday, I met Parker, Asher, and two additional brothers who were visiting from an affiliated church in southern Oregon inside Parker's living room for another study. At the study's conclusion, Parker sat across from me, smiling. "You need to get open about the past sins in your life if we are to proceed any further in your bible studies moving forward. I have an assignment for you," he continued, "I want you to write a list of all the sins you have committed in your life this week and be ready to talk about them next Sunday."

Did he want me to chew over every sin I had committed in my nineteen years of life? It felt weird to think about and divulge some sins I committed in elementary school. Would I even remember them all? I spent the rest of the weekend contemplating my sins, starting from the beginning.

The following weekend, we were back in Parker's living room again; I joined the four men huddled in a circle in the middle of the church's sanctuary—two random men on either side, Parker and Asher, directly in front of me. I had my handwritten sin list tucked away in my pocket. Parker uttered a quick prayer, and then he jumped into the mess of my life. "What do you have to confess? It's time to open your sin list and bear your life to us."

"Well I uh—"

I had no history with the two random brothers. Did they want me to get this vulnerable in front of them? The air felt warm, thick, and even sticky. But I took a deep breath and dove into the list. I divulged about lying and stealing and being overly vain. I confessed to cutting a neighbor's hose with a hatchet and starting fires as a seven-year-old. The confessions were uncomfortable, but the group made me feel like God was cleansing me.

Asher reassured me, "Everything is going to be okay, Kenny. The Holy Spirit is freeing you from your past. You're walking into the light."

I confessed to committing credit card theft.

"Keep going, Kenny. God is changing your heart!"

I rehashed my sexuality.

"That's it? That's all?" Parker asked, looking unconvinced, if not outright disappointed.

"Well, I did try to steal my friend's Gameboy back in elementary school."

"Yeah, yeah, we already addressed the stealing. Is there anything else?"

I sat up straight, feeling confident. "I guess that covers everything."

"I call your bluff! You, uh, ever masturbate?" He asked, looking at me with a devilish smirk.

"Do I what?"

"Do you mast-ur-bate?" He elongated the enunciation.

"Doesn't everyone do that?"

"How often do you masturbate, Kenny? Do you jerk off every night?" The questions were piercing a window into my private life. I remained silent, letting out a loud gulp. My throat felt dry from what felt like sudden, intense cardio.

"Well?" Parker demanded.

More silence.

Parker pressed further, "Do you want to burn in Hell for all eternity or not? You need to get open!"

"Dude, of course, I do. Everyone in the world does. What else do you want from me?"

"Kenny, I want you to imagine every time you lay in bed at night and begin to masturbate, you see Jesus nailed to the cross. Each time you stroke your dick, you are one of the Roman soldiers hammering a nail into Jesus's wrist. Each time you feel pleasure, you continue to his feet, hammering—joyfully—driving those nails deeper and deeper, blood splattering onto your face." He continued the discourse, pretending to masturbate by jerking his wrist next to his crotch. "Every time you ejaculate all over your chest and pillowcases," Parker said while pretending to cum, shaking and seizing, expressing an angry yet aroused passion on his face, his voice quivering before suddenly stopping and returning to a serious posture. "It's the death of Jesus Christ all over again!" He pointed at me. "You, Kenny! You are single-handedly crucifying your God and savior all over again! It's as if Jesus Christ died for nothing!"

Later that evening, we ate dinner and watched a gruesome reenactment of Jesus getting executed to show me exactly what my sin caused.

I replayed through a memory from cross country. I sprinted with my teammates up Beacon Hill near Minnehaha Park. Miss. Driscoll encouraged me to keep pushing as I jogged the decline of the hill, but I couldn't think of anything besides the pain. I felt hot, my calves were tight and achy, and I couldn't breathe—my stomach felt like it was being spaghettified. The workout, as I reflected, felt analogous to faith in Jesus. Maybe running hills was the archetype. "Why am I even doing this?" I yelled out toward the end of the workout.

Miss. Driscoll looked at me and shrugged. "Because no one else is." Her words glided through, a dagger to the soul. It was so simple yet so brilliant. How couldn't I have grasped it sooner?

At Starbucks, I let Asher and Parker know that I had decided to make Jesus the Lord of my life.

"There's the disciple in you we were searching for!" Parker sounded gleeful. "What brought you to this point?"

"It's kind of crazy, but God revealed something to me. Every day, I would show up to cross country practice. Long distance running felt painful, and sometimes I didn't want to keep going but I did. So yesterday I asked the question: 'Why do I want to live as a sold-out disciple?' It almost felt like God said to me, 'because no one else is!'"

"Alright, Kenny," Parker said. "We have one final thing to review before we can dunk you."

"Alright, shoot."

"Why do you feel like you're ready to be a disciple? Have you repented from all your sins?" The question caught me off guard. It felt accusatory and uninviting, not the welcome I expected when declaring allegiance to God's kingdom.

"Yes, I have."

"Alright, it settled. We look forward to welcoming you to the kingdom at your baptism." We all stood for a group hug. Truthfully, I hadn't fully repented in the way they expected me. But I was trying my best. I still felt distraught with my burgeoning homoerotic curiosity, but I didn't want them to know. Discipleship felt like an unattainable standard, but if I got baptized, I thought the journey would get easier; repentance would come naturally with time. Parker often preached perfection dressed in language, suggesting it wasn't possible. Still, I wanted to experience salvation. I would no longer be condemned to Hell when I died.

On our way back into Spokane, Asher drove us to a cliff overlooking the city. He stood next to me as we marveled at the scene. "You know this isn't an easy journey, right? One year in the kingdom is like ten years in the world. You don't grow a whole lot spiritually in the world."

"Yeah," I said.

The three of us sat silently, watching the sunset and reflecting on the journey ahead. Parker scheduled my baptism for Friday at the church building next to the community college in Spokane. Parker rescheduled Sunday service to accommodate members who wanted to participate in Bloomsday, an annual 12k race with over 50,000 participants yearly. It always takes place downtown Spokane on the first Sunday in May. I got baptized by the two men visiting from southern Oregon. Oddly, neither Asher nor Parker wanted to do the honors. The small gathering of Post Falls disciples clapped and cheered for me when I rose out of the water. Asher stood from his chair and led the entire assembly in song to celebrate the occasion—the salvation of another soul.

I sat with Asher in his car outside of my house. "What am I supposed to do with my sinful temptations?"

"Crucify them," he shrugged, kicking back a handful of assorted nuts. "You take the temptations to God directly through prayer," He said, chewing. "Pray for him to purify you and cleanse you from all unrighteousness. If you are struggling with temptations, especially sexual temptations, you're already in sin and need to ask for forgiveness."

"What about my attraction toward men? Will my spiritual journey get any easier?"

"Well, you could try dating in the church. Why don't you ask another sister on an encouragement date? It could lead to a joyful and fulfilling marriage!"

"Because I am not attracted to women. I've never been attracted to a woman once in my life. I don't see how it would help me. You don't understand what this feels like."

Asher leaned in close to me. "I understand well."

"You do?"

"I do!"

"How so?"

"Because I struggle with same-sex attraction like you do."

The Codependent Disciple

Asher was born into a devout Jewish family and raised in Tel Aviv, Israel. He relocated to the United States in his early twenties to attend Harvard University. But then he had a few run-ins with the law and was kicked out of the university nine months later. Around this time, members of a church near Lexington, Massachusetts, began influencing decisions in his life.

"You can say the Boston Movement saved my life," he said.

"The Boston Movement?"

"It's what the church used to be called before adopting the International Churches of Christ."

Asher never elaborated on what type of trouble he got into, only mentioning he should have gone to jail. He chose instead to focus on the ways God had changed his life. When the opportunity of a church planting in a new city came to his attention, Asher took it, and that's how he ended up living in Coeur d'Alene, Idaho.

Post Falls International Church of Christ only had roughly twenty members, so Parker and his Wife hosted Sunday worship in their living room. Parker and Asher routinely received ministry training in Spokane, so they drove over often.

Every Sunday afternoon, Asher picked me up for house church. He often regaled me with stories of his world travels in Indonesia, Germany, China, Taiwan, and even a day spent in North Korea—often reflecting on the cultures and their influence on his faith. Still, he made it a point to stick to his Jewish roots. Despite his proclamation of Jesus Christ as Lord, Asher had a Star of David tattooed on his left bicep and a sterling silver Chai necklace draped proudly around his neck. Asher also grew up wealthy, so he didn't need a job to survive, but he chose to work every morning at a local cafe to stay grounded. He always seemed intent on not being an idle body—he believed that no matter an individual's income level, disciples needed to be humble and work.

I viewed Asher as one of the most personable people I had ever met. He quickly became an intimate friend. He was—what the church called—my "discipler," the term used to describe one-over-one discipling. He was an accountability partner, except the accountability felt invasive and overreaching. Every morning, he expected me to confess to him whether I masturbated or looked at pornography the night before.

Since Asher jumped into my confidant and spiritual advisor role, he became only one syllable shy of my codependence. I felt intensely attracted to him, though I desperately tried not to. With each passing day, I grew more emotionally attached to him. I told myself he was my brother in Christ and nothing more. Who was I kidding? I wanted a sexual relationship with him. Did I need to confess this to him? Did these thoughts put me in sin as a result? I needed clarification.

After my baptism, Parker faded into the background of my walk with God. Since he focused on helping build up the Post Falls church, he appointed Asher as my shepherd, saying he would be my go-to man for everything. The church leaders expected every disciple to follow their discipler's example and seek their advice continually—about temptations, personal finances, and apparently, what I should study in college. Asher even encouraged me to avoid certain religious classes because they might hinder my faith. The subtle undertone of seeking advice or praying meant asking for the church's permission.

Make sure actions align with Asher's direction. Always ask for Asher's permission, I wrote in my journal.

Asher and I met four to five days a week and texted daily. Our friendship felt so intense, so magical. I loved every minute I spent around him. I could tell him that I loved him, but he would interpret it in a brotherly way. In return, he'd say he loved me—I sincerely felt it. I felt flirtatious around him. He had a way of making me feel like the most indispensable person in his orbit. I lusted after his body, but I tried to convince myself his fervent Godliness pulled me close to him. If anybody would get me to Heaven, Asher would.

Asher drove us to hike around Mount Spokane a few days after my baptism. This activity was his way of initiating my first D-time. The spring air felt crisp and chilly, with untouched snow patches from the winter and the smell of soggy pinecones.

"How's your faith after the high of your baptism?" he asked, crunching twigs and rocks below his feet.

"I'm doing pretty good. But I still struggle with lustful desires," I said. I wanted to divulge enough information but not the whole picture.

"That's normal, but you are stronger because of it."

I picked up a pine cone and attempted to kick it up with my foot. "Because of my sinful temptations?"

Asher joined in the game of hacky sack. "Because you chose to become a disciple."

He walked over to an empty bench covered in pine needles and motioned me over. After brushing the debris with our hands, we sat. Asher shifted the conversation. "You need to start looking for a job. You're an adult now. As a disciple, that means becoming a productive member of society, and you're not productive if you don't have gainful employment."

I told him I tried to get a job over the summer, but it never came to fruition. And it was true. I applied to Sky High Sports as a court monitor. I walked six miles roundtrip to the trampoline park daily, hoping the manager would finally interview me. He passed. Ninety job applications over three months were too much. But that was last year. Now, I was enrolled in classes full-time at the community college. I didn't have time for a job anymore, I said.

He let out a deep sigh. "Look, Kenny. Gone are the days of being part of this world. You need to be an upstanding and productive member of our church. Right now, you're being prideful and you need to look for a job." He pulled out his Bible and flipped the pages for scripture about the importance of tithing to the church and another scripture about pridefulness. Asher seemed to enjoy using the term "prideful" whenever we disagreed. But I needed clarification on what he meant by it. I didn't feel like I came across as prideful. But he knew his Bible better than I did. What gave me the right to protest?

"Fine, okay. I'll start looking for work this week," I said to appease him.

"Thank you, Kenny. I appreciate it when you listen to me."

We finished the hike by taking a selfie at a peak overlooking the State Park.

Nothing about Lilac City Gymnastics had changed in the last six years since my tryout—branded T-shirts and leotards displayed on the wall in the lobby. Flashbacks to my tryout and Dad's recounting of my rejection were making rounds. The gym owner looked at me. "My second interviewee hasn't arrived yet. Since you're early, I guess we can get started!"

I sat in the computer chair in front of the owner. "Sounds good to me!"

"Tell us a little bit about yourself?"

"Well, I am nineteen years old, and I graduated from Rogers High School last June!"

"And tell me, why do you want to coach at Lilac City Gymnastics?"

"Well, I am passionate about gymnastics, and it would be a lot of fun to have the opportunity to work with children! As a kid, I didn't have a chance to do gymnastics, so now I'm here, hoping to get involved as a coach!"

The gym owner asked me about my coaching style. I told her I was strict but fun. It felt like the correct answer to give.

Asher scheduled another D-Time, this time at a cafe called Red

Rooster, located next to Mission Park. Red Rooster was a unique coffee house operating within a former residential house. Did people who lived in the house fifty to one hundred years earlier ever think their home would someday convert into a coffee shop?

Asher pulled out a notepad. "How is everything going, Kenny?"

"Things are going well! I had a job interview at Lilac City Gymnastics!"

"That's great! Did you apply for any other jobs?"

"I didn't," I said, "but I was thinking if I get the job, I could train in the sport again, too!"

His joyful expression withered to a frown. He seemed appalled that I had only applied for a coaching position, even though it looked like a secured one. I clicked with my would-be boss. I wanted to know what the big deal was.

"You're being prideful again, Kenny! How are you expected to do great things for the kingdom of God being an idle body?"

My heart sank, and I could feel my body tensing. Something felt unfair about this conversation. I wasn't idle. Between school, church, and job hunting, I stayed busier than I had ever been before. He told me I could have applied for ten to fifteen jobs throughout my Saturday.

"God requires at least ten percent of your overall income!" Asher concluded.

He drove me back to my parent's house in silence. Once we arrived, he acted like it wasn't a big deal. "I have faith you'll get this job, Kenny." I stepped out of his car and walked toward my house, and he rolled his window down, "I really mean it!"

When I received the call from Lilac City to schedule my onboarding, I felt relieved. I had landed a coaching position. Whatever negativity I felt from our D-Time got replaced by the good news. I immediately texted Asher to share the excitement.

My phone rang right away. It was Asher.

"You need to tell them you need full-time hours. They might not schedule you much," he said as sternly as the day before.

Did I hear him correctly? Did he say he wanted me to work full-time hours, be a full-time student, and attend church functions throughout the week? D-Times with Asher were stressful and uninviting as if everything I did in my walk with God was wrong. It felt like I needed to do more to satisfy him. He never appeared entirely pleased. A power imbalance also complicated our relationship further. He was fifteen years older than me, so I often viewed Asher as my adult babysitter rather than my discipler.

A few weeks later, Asher picked me up from school for another D-Time at the Red Rooster. I greeted Asher in the parking lot as he sat alone in his car—window rolled down—hunched over his steering wheel.

"You in prayer there, buddy?" I asked.

"No," he said, looking up. "Mirabel broke off our engagement."

"Oh," I said, startled, unsure how to navigate the conversation. "I'm sorry to hear about that."

I wasn't sorry. I felt relief processing the news. Mirabel had exited the picture. Now, I could spend extra time with Asher. I tingled with warmth. I wanted to comfort him, though.

"Will you move in with me?" He asked, looking at me as I opened his car door. "I signed the lease to the apartment she and I would have moved into together after our wedding. But now she's gone!" Tears fell onto his lap.

"I'll need to think about it!"

"You will?" He perked up, tears paused, puppy eyes glistening. Was this the same man who cried moments earlier? His emotions shifted rapidly.

I knew I would answer yes; I wanted to live with him. The scenario sounded like a dream come true. After all, he was my best friend. There was one problem. We'd live near the Washington and Idaho state border and still needed a steady income from coaching to travel back and forth, let alone afford the rent. Asher had been right about Lilac City. The hours there were sporadic and noncommittal. The gym had only scheduled me to work on Thursday afternoons for about three hours as a substitute for a coach traveling Europe.

"How soon?" I asked. "I'm going to apply for a coaching position at Elite Gymnastics Academy."

"You could move in now if you want. I can cover the rent while you find stable employment," Asher said, fumbling for his phone. "Listen, I thought we could get a couple of brothers in the apartment and have a bona fide brothers' household! This living arrangement would help all of us."

The next afternoon, he invited me to view the apartment. The place looked clean and modern and smelled of fresh paint.

"You and I would share this bedroom and the other brothers," he pointed to the door at the end of the hall, "would share that bedroom."

Not only would we be living together, but we'd be sharing a bedroom. Asher didn't have to ask me twice.

Hoopfest weekend took place downtown Spokane. Hoopest, the world's largest three-on-three basketball tournament, attracts thousands of participants to Spokane annually. I never really got into it, but I enjoyed being in the hype. Asher and I were jogging through River Front Park, noticing all the shirtless men walking around dribbling basketballs.

"Oh man," I said. I tried desperately not to dwell on the mental images forming.

"My eyes will tend to wander at times, too," he said, "it's easy to want a second glance, ya know? You gotta pray to God about it as it happens."

"Or we can pluck both our eyes out, huh?" I joked, referencing a scripture in the Bible.

He chuckled, "for sure." We finished our jog, slowing to a walk about a block away from his car. "Purity is difficult for every follower of Christ. I have a book recommendation for you." Asher opened his trunk and pulled out a paperback copy of *Deep Convictions*, a workbook by the church's official publisher. "I also want to encourage you to also purchase a book called *Every Man's Battle*. You can read it alongside *Deep Convictions*. I think you'll get a lot out of them."

I thanked him, grabbing the thin workbook out of his hand.

Book recommendations, promoted through the church's official publishing house, were Asher's answers to my sinful nature. But I could barely get through a quiet time—roughly an hour of reflective bible study. Did he want me to complement my quiet time with another quiet time?

"It's crucial to fill our spare time with Godly activities or else we'll be tempted to walk into sinful situations."

I disagreed about filling all my spare time. But I couldn't argue with Asher. If I disagreed with him, he always had a way to back whatever he said with scripture. But I genuinely admired him because of his biblical knowledge. I saw him as the shining example of Godliness, a little too eccentric at times but perfect. I looked up to him as my spiritual idol and wanted to be half as faithful as him. However, his book recommendations sometimes felt condescending. Once, he mandated me to read *The Prideful Soul's Guide to Humility.*

Living with Asher turned out to be my fantasy fulfilled. It felt like the closest thing to a romantic relationship without the stress of living in sin. Our connection was brotherly and pure, or so I told myself. Whenever sexual energy sprung forth, I'd pray it away, talking to God about precisely how I felt:

Dear Heavenly Father, I wanted to come before you and confess my dirty thoughts toward Asher. I can't help that I want to have sex with him. He's so good-looking. Anyway, please forgive me for my sins, and thanks for letting me live with him. You're the best! In Jesus' name, I pray. Amen.

One night, Asher wanted to go out for drinks with friends he knew working at the Cafe.

"I'm going out for a drink with Jake and Sam tonight," he said.

"Can I come?"

"Well no," he wiped his sunglasses with a microfiber cloth. "You're still underage!"

I continued studying his movements. "Oh! Well, I thought we could stay in and watch a movie or something? How does that sound?"

"I want to meet with my friends. I haven't seen them in a while. I'll only be gone for an hour."

"Perfect! We can invite them here for a movie night!"

He picked up his wallet and stuck it in his back pocket. "We already made plans to meet for beers somewhere."

My pleas didn't affect any change in his plans. I pulled out the hysterics, trapping Asher like a crazy ex-girlfriend, runny mascara—the whole nine yards.

"Please don't leave!" I cried out

"Kenny, I need to get away from you for an evening, okay?"

I got defensive and rude, "Oh, You need to get away from me? You're going to go drink and drive home! How could you be so stupid? You could kill someone drunk driving!"

He walked toward the front door. "I'm not getting drunk. One drink is all!"

"No!" I yelled, running to block him. "You're going to crash and get somebody killed! What would God think about that, huh?"

Asher reached for the door handle. "Move away from the door, Kenny."

"Please, If you stay, we can have a D-time! We can talk about all my spiritual deficits!"

He tried to open the door; I blocked it with my foot. He lifted me like a toddler to move me out of the way. "I'm going whether you like it or not."

"Put me down!" I grumbled, trying to wiggle out his hands to block the door again.

He walked out the door and down the steps.

"I cannot believe you're going to sin against God, instead of staying here and being Godly!" I shouted from the porch.

"I'll be home in an hour, I promise!" He turned around, returned to the front porch, and touched my shoulder. "I'm sorry about what I said a few moments ago. I like spending time with you, but sometimes I want a night out. We can have a D-time and watch a movie when I get back. Okay?"

I spent the rest of the evening pacing around the apartment, mentally running through fake conversations and scenarios. How could Asher do this to me? When he returned home three hours later, he was cheerful and talkative. I felt betrayed, trying to calm myself.

"Three hours, Asher! Three! Not one like you said! Where have you been?"

"I'm sorry. I know you're upset. But can we talk about it in the morning? I, uh, I'm going to bed. You can, uh, come with if you want," He said, smirking.

I misunderstood the cue, climbing into my bed on the opposite side of our room.

"What are you doing?" He asked.

"Going to bed. You asked for me to come with you."

"Well—"

Everything about this moment felt so right yet so wrong all at the same time: lying next to Asher, naked in his bed, the warmth of his body pressed against mine, enjoying his chest hair pressed against my face. He laid back with his arms up, and I inhaled the smell of his armpits. I felt like a little volcano, ready to erupt at any moment. Suddenly, I understood something significant I missed early on when I met him: the feelings were mutual because he was guiding my hand onto his throbbing cock.

Starting Over

Oh, how I wanted more. Now that the intimacy faded, I kept replaying the scene. What happened stayed between Asher and me, yet somehow, I felt exposed to the masses, especially at church. If only we hadn't slept together. We had been living together for over one month when I finally gained the courage to pull him into the living room to discuss what had happened. "Can I talk to you for a second?"

"Yeah man, what's up?"

"I appreciate your friendship over the last year. You've become like a brother to me," I paused to think through my words, "but you and I are living in sin, and we need to repent."

I surprised myself with the confession. But we were in sin and not confessing it. I fell into sin, which meant my salvation was at risk. I would only continue to fall deeper unless I acted now. Asher sat on the couch, slouching forward. He looked at a loss for words before letting out a wheezing exhale. Did he feel regret?

"You're right, Kenny. We are living in sin," he said, "and this is my all fault. I'm sorry I allowed us to get this far into the world.

I'm supposed to help you grow in your faith and instead I've slowly been pulling you—well, us—into sin. I hope you can forgive me."

I told Asher I forgave him.

Our relationship had taken on a life of its own, and I felt helpless to stop the floodgates of romantic feelings I had for him. I felt powerless to stop what would inevitably come next: the fuck-around-and-find-out phase of discipleship. I would reap what Asher and I had sowed together. At first, I was optimistic about confessing our dirt and coming clean before him and God. But now the void took its familiar toll on my stomach, like the initial drop of a roller coaster. I wanted to take it all back. I wished I had never accepted his offer to climb into bed with him.

Confessing our sin brought me religious peace. I felt like God had forgiven me. However, the realization that I'd never experience the butterflies of a budding romance with another man was deafening. Had I been sentenced to a lifetime of celibacy and loneliness at baptism? My stomach turned sour—the anticipation of my future ran through my body like diarrhea.

Why did God create me? What was the purpose of God being omniscient and omnipotent if life were a choose-your-own-adventure? How could this all-powerful creator of my existence ask me to deny the innermost part of my soul? Why did God put me on earth if he knew I'd never cut it as his disciple? These questions cascaded through my mind. I felt horrified by God and afraid of what would happen next. I weighed the pros and cons. If I left the church, I could expect a fearful expectation of judgment—but I suppose I'd feel content on earth. If I continued as a disciple, however, I'd be forced to handle every heartbreaking aspect of denying a piece of my identity. But I'd be admitted into Heaven later. Both options gave me anxiety, so I fluctuated between hating God and hating myself for hating God. None of this felt honest or fair.

Despite Asher's emotional turmoil, I didn't expect him to have the strength and ability to continue living righteously. I thought our spiritual upheaval would simmer, and our friendship would return to normal. We might even rehearse another spiritual relapse or two before getting our act together to be holy before God. But he remained rock solid in his convictions, likely from the years he'd endured this brand of discipleship. I'd have to become calloused like him to commit to this lifestyle for the rest of my life.

Asher pulled me aside for another D-Time. "I spoke over the phone with the Campus Ministers in southern Oregon. They agree I should do the right thing and kick you out of the apartment."

I froze. "Kick me out? I've already paid you rent for the month."

"Yeah, but we can't expect to remain faithful servants of Jesus if we remain roommates. You'll also need to find a different discipler."

"What does this mean for our friendship?"

He turned around and entered the kitchen to grab his cup of coffee from the microwave. "I don't know, Kenny. But you need to leave. We need our time apart to grow and become spiritually healthy again. Another brother's household is starting in Spokane, and they might be willing to let you rent a room. "

I trailed behind him. "But what about the rent I already paid for this month?"

"What about it?" he sipped his coffee, "put your faith in God, and he'll work things out for you. But I do need to kick you out," he smiled. "Think about it this way—you won't have to rely on me for your daily commute to Spokane."

"You literally work at coffee shop in Spokane! Can I at least stay to get, you know, my rents worth of housing before you rudely kick me out?"

He set his coffee mug on the counter. "No, Kenny. Trust in God and he'll work everything out for you. Go check out the brothers' household."

Our friendship wasn't going to return to normal after all.

Parker began driving me to Post Falls and Coeur d'Alene for church events. On Sunday, I discovered all the juicy details of our sin had made rounds. Several men in the church knew what had happened. A brother I vaguely knew approached me, sipping his McDonald's coffee.

"I heard about what happened, which is weird because I didn't know Asher was... uh, you know," he said, extending a limp wrist. "He doesn't strike me as that. I hope you at least learned a valuable lesson! I'll pray for you both!"

I blushed. "Thanks."

"I think I know the source of your dilemma," he continued, "Asher was vulnerable after his breakup. But you? You aren't forming a relationship with any sisters in the church! Have you tried going on any encouragement dates lately? God can and does change hearts. Look at the ex-gay evangelist. That guy is a walking legend in the faith!"

"Who?"

"Some evangelist who is a former gay man. He has a whole ministry devoted to counseling same sex attracted disciples!"

Parker, who stood an earshot away, slid over and interjected, ever so friendly, "Are you scouting a potential discipler for yourself, Kenny?"

I wasn't.

"Come!" He smiled. "Let's go for a little walk."

I knew this smile. This smile communicated discipline. Parker marched us into his basement. Two other brothers were waiting in the wings.

"How are you this evening?" Parker asked.

"I am well," I said, "thanks."

"Good," he smiled. "Now, lets take out our bibles."

Parker's body language made me feel vulnerable. He crossed his arms, and all three men remained expressionless. I felt frightened by the vibe.

Parker stepped forward. "I knew partnering you two together would be a terrible choice. You know I saw this coming." He pressed his index finger against the pool table. "But because Asher is a strong disciple, and you looked so eager to become one of us. I said, okay, take a chance and let them spur one another onto love and good deeds. But I was wrong in my judgment!"

I sheepishly tried to defend myself, "I became weak and fell into sin. I'm sorry, I don't know what else to say."

Parker sneered. "Oh, stop being prideful!"

"I'm just supposed to struggle through this the rest of my life?"

"That's the call, Kenny!" He dug into me with his words. "Jesus never said discipleship would be easy! You and—Asher of all people—need to redirect your attention and focus on God if you want to live righteously! Wallowing in the loss of your sin isn't going to accomplish anything for either of you, and I refuse to show you both any sympathy regarding this situation. You two will have to reap the consequences of your actions!"

I didn't say anything. What could I say? I stood there in silence, taking their blows like the target of a firing squad. They accused me of having an evil heart, being a lover of sin, and not truly loving God. They accused me of being a false disciple. Were they treating Asher this way? They spent roughly an hour picking and prodding at the most vulnerable aspects of my humanity, tossing scripture at me like in the tampon scene from the movie Carrie.

To offset my situation's financial and emotional cost, I offered to coach extra recreational classes at Elite Gymnastics Academy. I needed the finances to cover another portion of rent into a separate household. But I also hoped coaching would distract me from the church's demands and the loss of Asher's friendship. Who knew Christianity would be so demanding? Asher and I were distancing ourselves emotionally, but despite the fallout, we were still part of the same ministry and routinely saw one another.

There were at least four required church meetings every week. I attended Sunday service, a meeting called bible talk on Tuesdays on the Northern Idaho College campus, and midweek on Wednesdays. We concluded the week at a devotional on Friday nights on the Northern Idaho College campus. I hoped coaching classes would be an excuse for skipping church events like Devo or Bible Talk. I found out afterward that it wasn't. Parker still expected me to be at all of the meetings. Teaching the extra classes at the gym further complicated my situation, and he admonished me to quit my job numerous times.

Meanwhile, Asher didn't so much as even acknowledge me whenever I came around. I could feel a jealous rage brewing like a hurricane. I hated watching him socialize with everyone else but me. He seemed so confident and flirtatious in all his interactions. A few days earlier, he showered me as the object of his affection and adoration. Now, I didn't seem to exist to him. Why couldn't I get over him? Did he move on already? He made it look effortless. I never expected his influence in the room to grieve me so viciously.

At Elite Gymnastics Academy one afternoon, I decided to train tumbling passes into the foam pit before teaching classes. Gymnastics would be the best way to release steam from the Asher debacle. When I practiced tumbling, I only had the skill before me to think about, not church or Asher. Independent gymnastics training after school became my new routine for several weeks. Every afternoon in the gym, I grew more confident in my ability to flip. But I still needed to improve my ability to twist those flips. I spent hours each afternoon attempting to teach myself a layout full-twist, getting lost and crashing into the blue blocks of foam each time.

I had spent four years with the Rogers gymnastics team trying to learn a layout full-twist—a backflip in a stretched-out position where the gymnast rotates a full three hundred sixty degrees upside down before planting their feet on the ground. Throughout my time at Rogers, my training was strictly rudimentary. I had yet to develop a concept of quality tumbling. My coach at the time, Kayla Kamerer, continued to drill the basics—the foundation I needed to be a successful tumbler, yet I fought against her advice.

"I want to learn a layout full-twist." I'd say.

"You can't even get into your back tuck properly, let alone do a layout. How exactly are you supposed to learn a layout full twist?" She'd respond, then give me some drills to work on that would have helped me had I listened. But Kayla was right; too often, I tried putting the cart before the horse. She had laid the foundation I brought to EGA, but I only realized the importance of it the day I began training under Aleksandr Sokolov and Chad Lopez. Aleksandr was tall, muscular in build, and tremendously flexible. Occasionally, he would jump into one-legged gainer-style backflips. Gymnastics differed from his background; he came from Martial Arts but had been coaching gymnastics for a few years and taught himself the basics. If anyone were the right coach for me, it would be someone like Aleksandr.

Chad was shorter but equally muscular. Unlike Aleksandr, gymnastics ran through his veins. He began coaching in the early 1990s. Both men augmented my training, offering me private lessons for nearly free. Aleksandr would create stations on the floor to help me better understand the air awareness needed for twisting. We'd use the trampoline and bring those concepts to the floor. Chad, however, could throw me into the air like a juggler. I often wondered where he got the confidence to spot gymnasts at this level.

At the beginning of my first private lesson with Aleksandr, he hurried onto the floor where I stood waiting for his direction. "Alright, you are going to run into a round-off, back handspring. Afterward, you'll dismount into a back pike, half twist."

"Easy enough."

Back pike, half twist.

The drills he gave me were to correct my amateur mistakes. I ran across the spring floor into a round-off, back handspring, launching into the air like a rocket. I promptly pulled my feet to the ceiling to get into the piked position. When I felt my body descending toward the ground, I twisted my hips and toes to the left side, inadvertently completing a full three-hundred-sixty degrees of rotation. My feet hit the mat with such force I had no choice but to fall backward.

"I just threw a layout full twist without thinking about it!" I yelped, bouncing off the floor to run a victory lap. Was gymnastics this easy once you figured out a technique?

Chad taught me a double backflip. The double backflip felt nothing like a layout full-twist. A double presented an opportunity to slam my head into the ground. Breaking my neck was possible if I didn't adequately train the skill. The double back felt more straightforward than twisting because there wasn't a variable to think about mid-flip. All I needed to do was get into position and hold tight until my feet found the mat. It was frightening. Because what if I didn't get high enough into the air? What if I land on my neck? One critical mistake, and I might never get to do gymnastics again. I grimaced at the thought of getting injured. But it was also exhilarating because I'd soon be capable of double backflips on the ground.

Learning to twist felt mentally taxing, but learning a double backflip felt physically challenging. As a result, during Chad's practice time, I wasn't strong enough to hold onto the shape of the flip against the gravitational forces. So, he aggressively conditioned me. Afterward, he spotted me while flipping my double back into the foam pit for several months. As I grew more confident, he added an eight-inch mat over the foam blocks for me to land on. After that, he placed the eight-inch landing mat on the spring floor and spotted me there. The first time I landed a double back tuck,

Chad looked at me and asked, "Are you ready to start putting together a full-in?"

That's a full-twisting double backflip. Aleksandr and Chad were crucial in helping me put together the skills necessary to compete as a level 10 floor and vault specialist. Did I feel ready to train at this level of gymnastics? Yes, I did.

My communications professor at Spokane Community College concluded the morning lecture. "Everyone is passionate about something," she said, looking around the room, "I want you to take time to reflect on where those passions could lead you in life if you wholeheartedly chased them. Your assignment will be a five-minute oral presentation."

My professor was familiar with my faith because I used her assignments as a platform to talk about it. Asher and Parker had previously ingrained in me the importance of making every conversation with members of the world fruitful to bring my hearers to faith, possibly even into our fold.

"Your faith in God is inspiring," she said after class, "you can tell when you talk about God how passionate you are. You really sparkle."

I must have been a passionate performer, like my faith in Christ appeared overwhelmingly positive—something keeping me going in the morning. And maybe at one time, it rang true. Now, my faith in Christ accomplished the opposite. It made me jittery and withdrawn.

I walked into the computer lab, and an idea formed. I sat down in front of an empty computer. What if I found a reason to move away from Spokane? If I moved, I wouldn't have to see Asher or Parker. What if I could train in gymnastics at the collegiate level? It seemed unrealistic because I had only been preparing for a short time. But I began learning a full-twisting double backflip. I knew what I would soon be capable of. I opened the browser to research colleges to learn about their men's programs. Did they accept walk-ons? What about gymnasts who specialize in one or two events? A Google search led me to a collegiate club program connected to all the colleges in the Greater Seattle Area. A website at the bottom of the page had the head coach's contact info. I could plan my move via my professor's assignment if I got accepted as a walk-on onto the team. It was brilliant.

I trained alone most days at EGA after school since Aleksandr and Chad were only sometimes available to coach me. The gym's silence provided a lonelier experience than I would have preferred. I stood at the edge of the floor leading to the foam pit to throw a full-in, hopefully landing the skill this time. I'd need the higher caliber skillset if I were to have any chance of success at the collegiate level. Still, doubt consumed me. I'd seen videos of college men's gymnastics. Why did I deceive myself into thinking I could measure up? I stood at the edge of the floor, staring at the eight-inch landing mat on top of the blocks of foam that saved my life countless times. I needed this skill. Out of the hundreds of attempts I'd taken that week, including precious ones taken with Aleksandr and Chad, I landed each try on my face. I didn't block enough during the take-off or lift my feet into the air swiftly enough to flip efficiently. It didn't occur to me that my strength and conditioning might be a factor. I didn't enjoy strength-based training. I had convinced myself that long-distance running and tumbling practice was sufficient.

I ran across the floor with a technique in mind Chad had taught me. I hurdled quicker and reached further into my round-off; my back handspring propelled me backward faster than anticipated. I quickly snapped tall and flung into the air.

Set, wait for the flip, initiate the twist, now PULL.

I felt uncertain, yet hopeful I would land this time on my feet.

Smack!

I felt the sting of the mat on my face. Eventually, I did land a full-twisting double backflip. I first landed the skill sometime in January of 2014. I grabbed my iPhone 5s to see if I could capture the moment again, but I only managed to land on my hands and feet like a baby for the rest of the practice. But I knew If I could land it once, I could land it again. Taking a full-in to my feet became the catalyst needed for writing the email that would determine my future in the sport.

The head coach of the college team got back to me right away. He said he'd save me a spot if I committed next season. Once I had a foot in the door, I began telling everybody I got accepted into a collegiate gymnastics program—everyone, except for church members, especially Parker, who had taken over as my interim discipler. I wasn't sure how he'd react to the news of me moving to the west side of the state. Would he be supportive of me chasing my dreams? I also didn't ask permission to see if it would be okay. There wasn't a smooth way to run this by him. I still set my plans into motion by giving my notice of resignation to EGA three months early. When I told my former boss I planned to move to pursue NCAA gymnastics, she congratulated me. I walked into the gym to start my independent workout and heard her call my name in the distance. "Coach Kenny!"

"Here!" I said.

"Are you interested in joining us for the Trampoline and Tumbling Demo on Saturday? We need a gymnast who can help demonstrate."

"Count me in!"

"Are you familiar with Trampoline and Tumbling? We are going to host the Trampoline and Tumbling Level 5-7 Nationals in addition to the U.S Elite Challenge in May and that's what this demo is all about."

"No, I haven't."

"Could be another avenue for you to train, you know, if you ever wanted to train after college." I kept it in mind, but I had no intention of joining a trampoline and tumbling team. The idea seemed less prestigious than men's artistic gymnastics.

Parker had become buddy-buddy with me again. He acted like our little fiasco in his basement never happened. I hadn't forgotten and didn't want to be his friend. In April, he ironically invited me on a trip to Seattle. I seized the opportunity since I had never been here before. But this trip felt like the right opportunity to fill Parker in on my plans. We rode into Seattle on a clear afternoon.

I tried casually bringing my plans to his attention while standing on the steps of the Mercer Island International Church of Christ, five minutes away from Seattle city limits.

"I'm moving here in July."

Parker looked at me, confused. "Here as in Seattle?"

"Correct."

"You what?" He snarled at me. "Why didn't you come to me about this sooner? You didn't even bother seeking advice before making such a rash decision!"

"I need advice from you and the church to move?"

"You don't want to risk becoming a fall-away, do you? Besides, it can be difficult for baby disciples to graft into another church. I need you to seriously pray about this decision before you ruin your life!"

"Well, I prayed about it. And I think it's the right decision for me."

"You're still an infant in your walk with God; you barely know how to pray correctly. You don't get to decide big decisions like this for yourself! This could hurt you spiritually."

"How exactly?"

"Do you think it's reasonable to stay grounded in our church if you move away while you're still new to the faith? It's tough to remain faithful if you don't have roots firmly established. It will be like starting over!"

I looked him in the eyes. "I'm not leaving the organization, I'm just transferring churches."

"Whatever." He said. "Suit yourself!"

The air felt cool and damp as the sun's warmth touched my skin. What did I have to lose? I would no longer be subjected to Parker or needlessly float around Asher's orbit. I knew the jealousy and heartache I felt for Asher wasn't healthy. Now, I felt like God was orchestrating my plans. After one visit to Mount Lake Terrace Gymnastics and the church, I felt confident I would be calling Seattle, Washington, home.

Something Isn't Right

Throughout 2014, I began feeling uneasy about the International Churches of Christ. I remember enduring an ungodly amount of required conferences and lectures—not to mention the time off work Parker guilt-tripped me into taking. In February, I attended the Mighty Men Warrior Camp. In March, the Missoula church hosted the Northwest Campus Retreat. Later, I volunteered at Teen Camp. By July, the campus disciples within the ICOC had plans to attend an event called the International Campus Ministry Conference (ICMC) in St. Louis, Missouri. I planned to skip the ICMC to save money since I was moving to Seattle.

During Bible Talk on campus at Northern Idaho College, Asher expressed different plans for me. "You won't be skipping the ICMC. All campus disciples are required to attend!"

Parker, who sat in a comfy chair, nodded in support.

I stood up, a feeble attempt at intimidation. "I'm moving in less than two weeks. I need to save money!"

"No... You need to attend the ICMC."

"I don't have—"

Parker cut me off. "Have faith in God. He will work things out!"

Faith in God, it turns out, was only a fundraising euphemism. Regardless of a person's financial status, Parker expected every disciple in the campus ministry to attend the ICMC. Asher hosted a fundraiser involving manual labor at the Tudor Revival home of a wealthy family in the church. We were there to help with various tasks around their property—picking weeds, planting small trees, digging out, and dragging big rocks across the yard from one garden to another. Upon entering the house, I imagined Cinderella coming down the staircase to help with the cleaning. What did these people do for a living to have two massive gardens? Tasks inside the house included organizing a library, painting walls, or scrubbing toilets with a toothbrush. By the end of the first day, I decided to return to EGA to coach a few summer camp shifts to raise the money needed for the trip.

I filled Asher in on my plan. As expected, he seemed less than enthusiastic. He asked me why I wanted to abandon the group. I explained. He pulled me aside and said, "You have a bad heart, Kenny! If you want to go on this trip, you must serve with the rest of us!"

I never wanted to go on the trip. Did I misunderstand him? "You and Parker both said this trip was mandatory."

"Kenny! I cannot believe you right now! You need to stop being selfish and think about all the good you are doing for God by serving. Be grateful this family is even paying you from the kindness of their hearts."

I stepped back. "That's the whole point—to pay for the ICMC!"

It wasn't just Asher; I felt a unified effort from the other four disciples in the campus ministry guilt-tripping me into staying, so I did, begrudgingly. At the end of our fundraising, I watched curiously as the house owner handed Asher a wad of cash, a thick stack of hundreds. Then he came over, gave me a twenty-dollar bill, and thanked me for the week of service around the property.

Before the trip, Asher demanded my twenty-dollar contribution, citing the gas bill for our drive to St. Louis. Twenty dollars wasn't nearly enough to cover the cost of transportation, so I assumed Asher held onto the rest of the funds for safekeeping. I was wrong. Despite fundraising, I still had to purchase my ticket to the ICMC in addition to my portion of the hotel expenses—money I didn't have, money I could have easily made teaching summer camps at EGA, money that I was supposed to have earned fundraising. It never occurred to me until recently that Asher might have exploited me for my labor.

On the first day, we drove seventeen hours in Asher's car toward the Midwest. Our first stop on the trip took place that night in Denver, Colorado, at the residence of a prominent family in the Denver Church. How were so many leaders in the ICOC so wealthy? We departed Denver the following afternoon and drove throughout the night across a cornstalk-smothered highway. We made it into Kansas City early the next day, and the sun blared through the windshield, blinding me as we continued eastward toward St. Louis.

We arrived in St. Louis around lunchtime. Checking into the hotel, I learned I'd be sharing a hotel room with Asher and his friend from another church, Alarik Sachs, who might as well have been an Andrew Christian Swimwear Model in Palm Springs. Like Asher, he looked equally jacked and spoke with a baritone voice that could cause the most proper to fall to their knees for forgiveness. How did the church even spiritually sanction this scenario? Why couldn't I have been paired with a former lesbian sister from another church? I couldn't imagine any promiscuous urges between the butch lesbian and the gay boy. The fight for personal purity was instantaneous.

Alarik started strong; I watched in lustful horror as he crossed his arms at the base of his shirt, pulling it over his head, revealing shredded abs and a happy trail merging into neatly manicured chest hair. Asher followed suit. Then, like little kids, they began rolling their shirts to whip one another as boys often do. Since I had no holy outlet for my needs, sexual vibrations plagued me. There was no way I would remain pure in my heart this weekend.

I pulled my bible from my bag and walked to a quiet corner of the room to read. I wanted to overcome this nightmare. Perhaps spending some time in the word of God might somehow keep me righteous for the rest of the weekend. I read from the book of Matthew:

> But I tell you that anyone who looks at a woman lust-
> fully has already committed adultery with her in his
> heart.

Well, that's just awesome, I thought. I had no doubt I fell into sin. But what could I do about it? Pray to God? I needed some-thing more to quicken me, to cut the sin out once and for all. I turned to the one bible verse I had committed to memory. Hebrews 10:26:

> *If we deliberately keep on sinning after we have received a knowledge of the truth, no sacrifice for sins is left, but only a fearful expectation of judgment and of raging fire that will consume the enemies of God.*

Did I want to be an enemy of God this weekend? I pulled Asher aside and spoke candidly. "You and Alarik are both causing me to struggle right now."

"How are we causing you to struggle?"

"You guys are literally walking around the hotel room half-naked."

Asher cocked his head, then looked toward Alarik. "You need to get open with him, man. Tell him about your sin, and we will proceed from there."

"You want me to confess this to him? Can you guys just not walk around in boxer shorts this weekend?"

"We can, but first, you need to confess! For the record, you're the one in sin, not Alarik or me! You need to confess your sin to him and repent."

"So, you're going to shoulder all the blame for this on me? How is this even fair? You know I struggle with this, Asher!"

"Ah, no. I struggle with this, too. You are just being prideful right now, Kenny!"

"I'm not the one walking around flaunting my body!"

I sat on the couch. "You're being prideful, Kenny," I mocked him quietly, then kneeled to pray.

Father God, please forgive me for my pride and bitterness. I am feeling weak in my faith right now. Please give me the strength to be righteous in all my interactions. In Jesus' name, I pray. Amen.

On the second day of the ICMC, I attended a lecture called Strength in Weakness hosted by an ex-gay evangelist. The ex-gay evangelist promoted Strength in Weakness (SIW) as finding strength in the weakness of homosexuality. Asher had strongly advised me to attend. SIW came to the rescue as the church's response to the gay issue. I sat in the first row, trying to look studious in my walk with God. The answer to my sexual orientation was choosing Jesus instead of LGBTQ desires every day, the ex-gay evangelist said from the pulpit. Discipleship was about wholly surrendering my life to God's will. As I remember, we were encouraged to create an SIW social media account through the official website. The account offered me daily bible reading and connected me with two men who counseled me regarding my unwanted same-sex attraction.

Later in the evening, Asher pulled me aside before going downstairs to where a large group of disciples formed in a flash mob, singing hymns and worshiping God. "I'm sorry for how I treated you earlier. I wanted to share a room with you because I do like you and would like to spend some time with you before you move away. I can find you a different room with someone else, if you'd like."

"No, it's fine. I can stay. Let's just get through this weekend." I said, trying to sound annoyed at his advance.

The way he smiled suggested he knew how I felt. The truth is, I wanted to be with him, too. I hated him, but I was smitten with his masculinity. Moving away from Asher was the only logical decision if I wanted to remain faithful to God. I viewed Seattle as the future promised land where my faith would flourish. I began mentally preparing for the heartbreak. Through all of this, he was still the man of my dreams. He was the man I wanted to build a life with, but it wasn't feasible. Not if I wanted to remain irreproachable as an ICOC member. Not if I wanted to make it to Heaven. What would my life be like without him? I reflected on the strength I drew from him to be firm in my convictions. Homosexuality was a sin; there was no doubt in my mind—I had no choice but to move on, make peace with the past, and find renewed hope as one of God's chosen followers.

Back in Spokane, Asher asked me to hang out the night before my flight to Seattle. He apologized and said he wished our time together could have ended differently. "Your friendship has meant a lot, Kenny. I hope you find inner peace on your next adventure in the Emerald City. I'll continue praying for you." His eyes sparkled in the moonlight. I wanted him to grab me, pull me close, and shove his tongue down my throat. But he didn't. Instead, he leaned in for a side hug and dropped me off at my grandmother's house. I never saw him again.

Moving On

The Northwest Christian Conference kicked off my status as a Seattle resident. It was a smaller conference for all the affiliated ICOC churches in the Pacific Northwest. It wasn't memorable, mainly the same information received the weekend prior in St. Louis. Don't be gay, deny yourself pleasure, be faithful, follow Christ, be miserable, jump off a bridge—oh, and there was lots of cheerful singing. I used the conference as a springboard to launch headfirst into the church. I lodged with a group of brothers who lived in a house in Queen Anne next to Seattle Pacific University, a short distance from the Seattle Center. The brothers and I chewed over our testimonies and personal struggles, read our bibles, and prayed together. Sometimes, it felt like I was the only brother in the ministry who struggled with same-sex attraction. Maybe it was for the best. I couldn't afford to get drenched in another homoerotic scandal. I needed to stay focused on God to keep my salvation. Jesus Christ and my devotion to the church came first. Everything else was secondary, including gymnastics.

Who was I kidding? I knew I had moved to Seattle to pursue gymnastics. But I tried convincing myself my focus was on God. During gymnastics practice, I'd attempt to indirectly share my faith with my teammates, whom I only viewed as potential converts to the church. I regarded every outsider I met as such, even implementing love-bombing tactics I had learned from Parker and Asher. I had to because growing the church membership was the primary goal. It hinged on the scripture written at the end of the book of Matthew about going into the world and making disciples of all nations. Was I spiritually healthy if I wasn't making disciples? If I kept my focus on God by making disciples, I believed God would bless my journey in gymnastics. The sport gave me the courage to remain faithful to the church. Life already felt like a battle for God's wavering approval based on how well I did spiritually. Juggling God's standard of perfection with my unquenchable desire for humanity was at the forefront of each day. I often felt like I was drowning; I didn't have the strength to focus on making disciples because I struggled to be a disciple myself.

Training in gymnastics felt tangible; it gave me hope. Training became a reprieve from the daily grind of participating in bible talks, D-times, confession of sin, midweek service, Friday night devotionals, Sunday service, random prayer walks, warrior prayer nights, and cold contact evangelism. The church subtly laid out these activities as a membership expectation, in addition to remaining holy and perfect. I couldn't keep pace with the stringent purity culture and lordship salvation without hope in something different than Heaven in the afterlife: gymnastics filled the gap. Gymnastics not only anchored me to my faith but to my academics at Seattle Central Community College as well.

I moved into Charles Langford's house on the North end of Capitol Hill, a mansion run by Seattle disciples in the campus ministry.
Charles only charged one hundred dollars a month for rent and a
full day's worth of household chores, so I took a part-time coaching
position at King County Gymnastics to make ends meet. Charles
was a thirty-four-year veteran of the ICOC, an early tech pioneer
to account for his wealth. Mitch Marseilles, one of the roommates
in the house, introduced himself as my discipler, greeting me with
a side hug. We had never met, let alone discussed the possibility
of moving forward with the relationship. But here he was, taking
ownership of my life as if making a stock market trade.

"This will be your room," he said while taking me on a tour of the
creaky old Victorian home. "I'll let you settle in for a bit. Charles
will host a household Devotional around six p.m. Be sure to come
meet everyone when you're unpacked." The room was spacious,
with a large window to the backyard and a huge closet. I brought
only a few items to Seattle with me. I didn't need all the space.

Upon my arrival at Mount Lake Terrace Gymnastics Academy,
I noticed the college boys on the team were rowdy and trained
shirtless. My battle with lust toward them, I noted, would be ongoing. Especially since I didn't have the leeway to talk to them and
say something like *hey, I get horny watching men parade around
half-naked. Horniness is a sin, and sin will lead me to Hell. Could
you cover your body for me, please?* During practice hours, I enter-

tained leaving the church to pursue a relationship. But I didn't feel like I could confess this sin to Mitch. If I did, his advice—which would have effectively been a command—would be to cut gymnastics out of my life. He'd tell me gymnastics hindered my relationship with Jesus. Mitch kept tabs on every aspect of my life, even more so than Asher did. Instead of impurity and repressed sexual urges, I confessed about the godly conversations I'd engaged with my teammates. I also mentioned how unfruitful and discouraging it was. I needed to sell the illusion of trying my best.

"I don't feel like I am getting anywhere. I am not making a godly difference on this team!"

"You won't see results overnight," Mitch said, "continue to have faith and go to God in prayer. Remember, it's not your job to convert anyone; you're only planting seeds. God waters and lets them grow into a faith of their own."

I remembered the conference I attended in Missoula in March. The evangelist had preached a powerful message that infected me. His final sentence of the afternoon had become my slogan. *Igniting faith in others will fan your faith into flames.*

I prayed to God for faith among my team. I wanted to experience the superiority of baptizing a new member. It wasn't enough to be a church member; you had to be a cog in the disciple-making machine. A successful Bible study appeared to other church members as a seal of righteousness. It communicated how spiritually healthy a disciple was. Still, it always felt like the same three or four people were the only ones making a difference in God's Kingdom. Despite wanting to make a difference in the world, I cringed and grew flush in my attempts to talk about Jesus with outsiders. Jesus was a taboo subject, especially if I came across as preachy instead of philosophical and open-minded. At the gym, I opted to continue my indirect evangelism techniques because I hoped forging friendships would serve as the perfect segue to discuss my journey into Christ.

One afternoon before practice, I walked to the grocery store across from the gym and purchased a giant case of Gatorade. I attached a scripture from Psalms to each bottle that read, *"A generous person will prosper; whoever refreshes others will be refreshed."* I couldn't wait to start helping these boys make it to Heaven. The longer I stayed on the team, however, I ceased fitting in with the group. I was an introverted, soft-spoken Christian boy who equated any physical affection, except the all-inclusive side-hug, with a sin. I was also one of the least talented gymnasts in the group. The level of gymnastics some of these boys brought to the team blew me away. I was genuinely shocked at how talented they were. Owen, my teammate from New York, and I vaulted together during practice. "Have you watched Blue Mountain State?" He asked.

"No, I haven't? Is it funny?"

"It's hilarious, dude! You need to watch it and let me know what you think!" He said before sprinting head-on into the vault table, throwing a Yurchenko double twist. It was mesmerizing to watch an elite-level vault in person.

I wanted Owen to experience my faith. At home, I watched an episode of Blue Mountain State, searching for a reason to shut it off. I would attempt to cut Owen to the heart. I wanted to show him that Blue Mountain State did not please God. I could offer some biblical advice to help him live a life pleasing to Jesus.

"I turned off the show within five minutes," I told him the next day at practice. "I couldn't allow myself to watch such filthy content and be on amicable terms with Jesus."

Owen gave me a weird look. "Uh, Okay," he said, walking away.

I'm sure my prude nature solidified my reputation on the team. I imagine Owen viewed me as a brainwashed Jesus freak, unable to think or decide for myself. Since assuming the role of Team Christian, I had converted no one, and now I began looking like a religious fanatic. Still, I hoped I could break at least one of these boys, invite them to church, point out their sins, and convince them to turn their lives over to Jesus for eternal salvation. When Owen returned, he asked, "would you get in trouble for falling short of these standards set by your church?"

"I mean, yes," I said, "but it's always out of love to help us grow in our faith. The standards are set by the bible, not the church. We simply live as the bible commands."

"That doesn't sound healthy at all."

"I'll agree, it does sound like an impossible wall to climb, but it's worth it!"

"Is it, though?" He squirted a little honey onto his hands and rubbed them together so they wouldn't slip mid-flip off the table.

Was I evangelizing Owen, or was it vice versa? He made a valid point.

"Uh..."

"Has it been worth it so far?" He asked again before sprinting toward the vault table.

Well, not exactly, but in the end?

Strength in Weakness

I integrated the principles of Strength in Weakness (SIW) into my daily life. Often, SIW was challenging to process, sad, even. I once heard an ex-gay evangelist say that no temptation is permanent and that God promises relief. Except that it wasn't true. Not for me, at least. My temptations were growing stronger and louder. Still, I felt inspired to walk the walk as a Christian. Being part of the ICOC made me feel superior, encouraging me to keep moving forward. SIW touted itself as a ministry that bridges the gap between Christians and LGBTQ members through "awareness, education, and support." Though a proud member, I didn't feel like the ministry was building me for success. I still struggled to overcome my homoerotic temptations. SIW didn't publicly declare itself as anti-LGBTQ. It alleged compassion and understanding while, in the same breath, asserting the biblical design for sex and intimacy as reserved between a man and woman bound in marriage. All I did as a member was suppress my sexuality. Suppression was the primary support the ministry enriched me with. What I didn't understand was I had actively involved myself in Sexual Orientation and Gender Identity Express Efforts—I was oblivious to my participation in what others have deemed conversion therapy. But here I was, at another conference, sitting at a breakfast table with an ex-gay evangelist—one of the leaders in SIW.

Kenny Strange 10/26/13
To: ████████████████ & 1 more >

████████████████████

Hey! My name is Kenny Strange, I'm a 20 year old male, I've been a disciple for roughly 5 months and struggle hard core with homosexuality. It's kind of just always there reminding me of how broken and hopeless I am. I've got a really close friendship with a certain ██████████ you may know him, he suggested that I email you and get help... I also read Caring Between The Margins a while back. Anyway, I want some info on the Strength in Weakness Ministry.

An email I sent to an ex-gay evangelist. My introduction to the organization.

Disciple A., another well-known brother in the ICOC, mingled in the same room. We had only briefly chatted at breakfast before I made my way down the hall to find my seat in the front row of the lecture hall, where he and the ex-gay evangelist would both be speaking. Before the lecture, I only knew of Disciple A. because the ICOC spread his testimony church-wide. He formerly lived as a transgender woman. While studying the Bible, he decided he was ready to live as a man again. I found his testimony highly inspirational. How did he have the courage to do it all? Struggle not only with unwanted same-sex attraction but also unwanted gender identity? I felt grateful I only dealt with one issue. I could only imagine how he felt waking up in the morning. I assumed God was pleased with his efforts to suppress two major innate, unalterable pieces of his existence.

I joined Strength and Weakness because Asher kept nagging me about the organization. He said the ministry helped him curb his unwanted same-sex attraction and explore the possibility of sex and intimacy with a woman. Something didn't add up, though. Did SIW help Asher? There's no way; otherwise, he wouldn't have slept with me. Did his engagement end because of his attraction toward men? I could only speculate. Questions were forming regarding my situation. I wanted to know how to remain strong enough to keep fighting. My battle felt messy and debilitating. While listening to Disciple A. speak, I noticed his confidence seemed shaky. His voice maintained uncertainty when discussing his transgender detransition. I could see that Disciple A. had become an empty shell of the woman he used to live happily as. Whenever he spoke, it appeared he wanted to sell an illusion that their detransition was a gift given by the grace of God. Was the ministry about taking individuals and hammering them with the Bible, fitting them into a mold they were never supposed to fit in?

I supposed I felt the same way as he did. I often spoke about my relationship with Jesus as if it were a transaction. I touted following

Jesus as the most significant decision I ever made. Deep down, I wanted out. I wanted to feel happy, and discipleship wasn't cutting it. The defining factor stopping me and every member of SIW from going back into "the world" was the same: fear of judgment in the afterlife. Members of the ICOC and SIW told me on many occasions—directly quoting Philippians 2:12—to work out my salvation with fear and trembling. SIW never gave me a definitive answer of what to do with my unwanted sexual desires besides the cookie-cutter responses, like creating boundaries or praying about it.

When I studied the Bible with Parker, he once told me that a person's faith and physical body were two different aspects of their humanity. Whichever piece a person chooses to feed will be the strongest. He equated the two elements to two fighting dogs; one dog got fed steak and chicken every night, while the adjacent dog starved. Which dog would be victorious in a fight? I nourished my spirituality, yet I continued growing hungry for promiscuity in the LGBTQ community. I reasoned it was because I killed those carnal desires daily. Maybe Parker was right. My faith would overcome in a battle against my flesh. I would be victorious in the fight against my sexuality if it came to it. All I needed to do was fight.

I felt inadequate as a gymnast and disciple. The two systems demanded perfection. I felt like I was failing God, my team, and myself. I couldn't convince any of my teammates to come to church with me, and I had become a pariah among the group. They were all young twenty-somethings who lived carefree lives. They didn't have heavy expectations of church membership. They didn't have somebody else's salvation held over their head like I did. My duty was to do everything I could to save them, yet nothing I did brought them any closer to Jesus Christ.

My coach's expectation for my commitment to the team also shifted as he began preparing for the upcoming competitive season in December. He wanted me to start training full-time with the rest of the team, ending closer to nine p.m. each day. Since I only planned to compete in two events, I usually completed a short conditioning workout after finishing the vault and floor rotations for the evening before catching the bus home. This conflict with gymnastics would cause me to miss two of the four central group meetings throughout the week—Bible Talk and Devo. I brought the issue to my Campus Minster, Jacob Bosman.

"I'll need to skip bible talk and Devo over the next couple of weeks."

Jacob looked at me incredulously. "Why do you need to miss these vital meetings with the body?"

"My coach switched around my training schedule at the last minute. I am going to talk to him about the situation to get back to my regular training hours since I will only compete in two events."

"Let him know you're active in church and can't afford to miss meetings with the body," he started walking away toward his wife, Sarah, while maintaining eye contact. "A spiritually healthy disciple is a physically healthy athlete!" He yelled from across the sanctuary.

In addition to the training hours at Mount Lake Terrace Gymnastics, I discovered the team had to raise money in the fall and spring months to keep the program running since the NCAA did not fund it. The fundraising efforts were always on Sunday during church. I dissociated as my coach broke the news. Why was this happening? Why would God bring me to Seattle only to watch me crash and burn? I had to let my coach know I couldn't attend the fundraising.

I exercised caution, hoping he would be understanding and supportive. "I can't join the fundraisers on Sundays. I have church."

He looked away from the guy's training release moves on the horizontal bar. "This is a mandatory part of being on the team. If you want to compete, you'll need to pull your weight by helping fundraise."

"But my church isn't going to allow me to skip out on these meetings, though."

"Fundraising will only be for a couple of months. We may need to rethink your place on this team if you can't commit, Kenny."

My heart dropped. "Okay, I'll talk to my church and see if I can make it work."

I had to fight for what I wanted. I had to let someone know I had another schedule conflict. I wanted to avoid the looks of bewilderment and disdain from Jacob or Mitch as I bailed out on the most critical meeting of the entire week.

This time, I touched base with Sarah. "My commitment to gymnastics is forcing me to temporarily sacrifice Sundays to help fundraise to support the team."

Sarah tilted her head slightly. "I see. And how long would this last for? I hear from Jacob you are already skipping out on several meetings with the body. Is this true?"

I slumped my shoulders, but I still wanted to sound optimistic. "It's true. This should only last a couple of months."

She made me feel like I wasn't acting faithful enough to the church to be considered a true Christian. "You'll need to consider your allegiances seriously. With gymnastics or with God?" She continued. "It sounds like gymnastics is getting in the way of your relationship with Jesus, and I'm concerned for your salvation at this point."

Mitch must have caught wind of my situation through John and Sarah. He later scheduled a D-time with me at Starbucks. "How's your faith?"

"It's great!"

"Well, that's not what I've been hearing. I need you to be honest with me."

"What have you been hearing? Is this about skipping church on Sunday? My faith isn't the issue here. I'm having a tough time juggling my schedule."

"Your faith doesn't seem genuine enough to effect any change in those who encounter you. All you seem to care about is gymnastics. It's looking pretty fruitless in your walk with God." He said, looking at me from across the table. "Are you regularly evangelizing?"

My world felt like it was falling apart. My discipleship threw a wrench in the cog. My dedication to gymnastics led the church to view me as not devoted enough to Jesus. My commitment to the church led my coach and team to view me as uncommitted to gymnastics. I stood in the middle of an uncomfortable gridlock.

One afternoon before practice, my coach approached me. "There is nothing wrong with having faith or being part of a church," he threw a block of chalk over to one of my teammates. "But to be part of this team, you must make gymnastics the number one priority in your life. I want you to take the week off from the gym to clear your head and think about what's most important in your life. Is it gymnastics or being an active member of your church?"

What was it going to be? I couldn't believe this was what my commitment to the church would distill down to. In those early months after my baptism, Asher repeatedly told me that God would sometimes call me higher in my faith by abandoning worldly passions, even when it hurts. According to Asher, these were a test of character and loyalty. So, what was it going to be? Gymnastics or my faith? My salvation and the fear of going to Hell were too strong to walk away from this church. Worse—amid the chaos, I had fallen behind in my classes at Seattle Central. The workload felt too colossal for me at a time like this. I withdrew from all my courses and returned to the gym to break the news. I was dropping out of college and walking away from gymnastics.

At a Friday night devotional, I told Mitch I had decided to step away from gymnastics to focus on God. He patted me on my shoulder. "Hey. Listen, Kenny. This is fantastic news! I know it was probably painful, but I promise you made the right decision." He stood in front of the room. "Can I have everyone's attention for a second?" He waited for the talking to stop. "Listen, my man Kenny here, who came to Seattle to pursue college gymnastics, has decided to walk away from the sport to focus on his commitment to God."

One person began clapping, and then another person joined. It started as a slow clap erupting into a thunderous standing ovation from every member of the campus ministry. I felt momentarily overjoyed by the applause, blinded even. The experience took my breath away, but the joy didn't last long. To the disciples in the campus ministry, I looked like a dedicated Christian renouncing the worldly to focus on treasures in Heaven. To me, I felt like I received a death sentence. What was the purpose of this life on earth? Was it to continue living a rigid and tightly controlled life as a disciple to earn enough brownie points to make it to Heaven after I died? Was the God of the universe worth this pain? The standing ovation was a temporary and fleeting spiritual high. I would need to keep reminding myself through scripture and meditation that, in all things, God remained in control.

Ellis no longer wanted me to occupy a space in his house, rightfully belonging to another disciple who might need cheap lodging while in school. Since I withdrew from the campus ministry, he wanted me to find a brother's household to live in. Depressive episodes took hold of me—I slept late into the afternoons and abdicated my weekly chores around the house. I began spiritually spiraling, turning into an increasingly terrible roommate, which likely fueled Ellis and Mitch's push for me to find another place to live. Late one night, I decided to dig deeper into the church's history. The top video on Google was a YouTube link calling the church organization a cult. Barbara Walters introduced viewers to video footage of John Stossel's undercover investigation. His findings highlighted experiences similar to my own in the church. Were these experiences abnormal? Had I been recruited into something entirely different from biblical Christianity? Was I brainwashed by a quasi-Christian church operating under the guise of truth to benefit church leaders? I couldn't have been that vulnerable, right?

I brought my suspicions to Mitch the next day. "Are we in a cult?"

"That's a common attack on the church. But no, I don't believe so. We are persecuted as a church because we live out God's word daily. Satan doesn't like that, so he attacks the church through those types of accusations." He pulled out his Bible, "Here the Bible says, 'Be alert and of sober mind. Your enemy the devil prowls around like a roaring lion looking for someone to devour.' You see, Kenny? Does this make sense? The devil is an accuser, and that's what he is doing to God's church."

"Yea, I guess. There's a lot of information out there suggesting we are."

"If you're struggling, it means you're in the right place. Keep fighting the good fight. At one point in our church's history, we were on the number one FBI Cult Watch List in America. Satan wants to destroy us and will use anything he can to attack us. Don't let him plant seeds of doubt in you. You're a child of God."

"Child of God or not," I said, "biblical discipleship feels unbearable at times."

"While I don't fully understand your specific struggles, I understand sin. We all go through it. I'll pray for you."

Life as a church member grew exponentially more physically and emotionally taxing. Mitch became a staunch advocate for my continued engagement in SIW. But I began romanticizing my escape. I wanted to pursue a relationship with another man. I was needlessly tired in my walk with God. Why did I feel so hopeless? Why did I feel so unhappy? If I left the ICOC, I would be labeled a "fallaway." I feared I would lose my friends and be alone in the city. All of my friends were in the church. The ICOC had cut me off from the outside world. The organization hijacked my faith and left me with nowhere to run. My conclusions about the church were calcifying.

The more I researched, the more I saw the ICOC for what it was—a pyramid scheme in the form of Christianity—the various leaders filtering down to the rank-and-file members at the bottom. The church presented a numbers game. Did I bring enough visitors to church? Did any bible studies materialize from those visitors? Did I pray enough? How much did I tithe of my overall income to the church? Did I remember to give an additional percentage of my income to the "special" contributions for the week, too? The amount always felt unattainable, especially in a city like Seattle. All the obligations to the church had chipped away my faith and brought me to suicidal ideation. It felt like the only way out.

I confided in a coworker at King County Gymnastics about my situation. I sat on the floor next to him as we put our shoes on after Open Gym ended. "I am discovering maybe there is something sinister lurking underneath the image of my church. I am struggling with making the correct decision in my walk with God."

"Sounds simple enough to me. Why don't you just leave?" He said, packing his sweats in a bag.

"I don't want to go to Hell."

We exited the gym and walked toward his car together. "Do you believe you'll go to hell for this?" He added, "also, do you need a ride?"

"Yes and yes."

He drove us down toward Capitol Hill, "I can't decide for you, but it sounds like, well, not a very good situation. Are you going to let this church dictate your life? Why don't you download Tinder or Grindr and see if you match with a guy? You live in one of the gayest cities in America."

Once I got home, I took his advice and downloaded the apps. I opened Grindr before service that Sunday, hoping another brother in the church might stand in the same boat as me. There wasn't. Instead, Mitch, who sat in a pew talking with other members, saw me and came over to say hello. I brought my feelings to his attention. The advice he tried instilling in me was the opposite of my coworker's. "Why don't you ask a sister on an encouragement date? You could both fall in love!"

"Another encouragement date with a sister? That's your solution?"

"Well, God could change your heart. Plenty of members in Strength in Weakness are in long lasting marriages."

I raised an eyebrow. "But are they happy? I don't feel like you understand the gravity of the situation."

"No, I don't understand your situation, but you're severely limiting your faith. God can't work on a hard heart like yours! Like I already said, plenty of same-sex attracted disciples are in happy marriages to the opposite sex. Have faith in Strength in Weakness."

"Well, I'm not happy. I'm giving everything I have to remain faithful, but this feels impossible."

"Listen, there's nothing I can do for you. In the meantime, I'll keep you in my prayers."

I stood aloof in the back of the church's sanctuary. I no longer pretended to be joyous in my walk with God. I began wondering if the ICOC had covertly tricked me into following a set of systemic unbiblical practices. Was this the reason I felt miserable? Or was Satan trying to pull me back into the world? Was the pyramid scheme design of the church part of God's unblemished design? What if the outside influence surrounding the ICOC's label as a cult was indeed an attack by Satan? This couldn't be the result of manipulation and brainwashing, could it?

I began coming to terms with the situation, but I still felt incredibly doubtful of the church's label as a cult. The ICOC First Principles Studies, which Asher and Parker had diligently walked me through back in Spokane, seemed airtight. Everything I read in the Bible squared away with how I saw church members live their lives. Deep down, l still grappled with uncertainty, so I second-guessed myself. The one thing I knew for sure, without a shadow of a doubt—I couldn't bear to suppress my sexuality any longer. I began turning to suicidal ideation as a coping mechanism, maybe even comfort. What if ABC 20/20's assessment of the church was accurate? Worse, what if it wasn't? Ultimately, I continued believing the church was perfect, and the problem was me. But I still wanted out. I needed out if I were to remain alive.

I examined the church-directed decisions I made over the last few years. I had been in conversion therapy for two years. I had tossed gymnastics into the proverbial waste basket. I even dropped out of college. Had all these decisions been worthwhile? Was my faith in this church all for nothing? Where was my faith taking me anyway? Why did God seem absent in all my misery? Early in my discipleship, I believed I had made the correct decision, but now I wasn't so sure. On my walk home, it began to sprinkle, and then a complete downpour of wind and rain fell on top of me as I stood on the 130th Street bridge overlooking Interstate 5. I screamed out at the traffic racing below me like a raging river. I wanted to jump off, but I was afraid of death. I feared what God might do to me if I followed through. Instead, I caught the bus home, sat on my bed soaking wet from the rain, logged into my Facebook account, and penned a short message for everyone in the church to read.

This Facebook post is my official resignation from the International Churches of Christ. I no longer wish to live my life as a disciple of Jesus Christ.

1

---

1. Strength and Weakness publicly denies the support and use of conversion therapy. But the ministry's whole purpose, in my experience, seems to be to convince LGBTQ people that our identities require a consistent effort to repress them. If not conversion therapy, then what do we call it?

Capitol Hill

Seattle

Unaware

The nebulous religious structure of my childhood had taken its final form in my decision to get baptized into the International Churches of Christ. The organization exasperated my childhood fears as a member and—as I would soon find out—for an additional five years post-resignation. Sold-out discipleship not only emotionally maimed me; it petrified me. As I entered the world with a renewed sense of mission and purpose, I could almost feel the flames of Hell trailing behind me, ready to gulp me at a moment's notice. Who was I now that I no longer lived as a disciple? Apparently still a disciple. My internal monologue carried along precisely as the ICOC had taught me. I had no way of unlearning the indoctrination. I didn't see a need; I believed the ICOC taught unadulterated truth.

My beliefs were intrusive, and I kept them to myself. I mean, I had to—if I wanted to fit in. I didn't want to believe I'd go to Hell. But I no longer devoted my life to the church, and that notion was precisely what my rejection of the ICOC meant. So, there I was, slandering the church. I wasn't a member anymore; why did it matter? Did I label the church a cult because I rejected what I believed to be the truth? Or did I overcompensate for my inability to live faithfully, perhaps even parroting what other ex-members called it? Did I think the church was a cult? Internet searches raised my awareness, but many disciples made me believe my anger arose because of my lack of faith. ICOC members had placated me into thinking my sin was the problem.

Perhaps my sin would help carry me to restoration back into the church. I viewed my upcoming lifestyle choices as the starting point for my eventual return to the ICOC. The consequences of my newfound hedonism would be the turn of events waiting in the wings that would bring me back to the foot of the cross. But for now, the next logical step for me to take would be to break free from the church for a time—experience immorality and drunkenness, and then I'd realize my dire need for repentance, propelling me back into the fold. I'd even have a killer testimony on how Jesus brought me back.

I left the International Churches of Christ in mid-September 2015. By October, I began mentally preparing to walk into a gay bar for the very first time. I learned about Seattle's Capitol Hill neighborhood through my coworker, who introduced me to the LGBTQ apps. Now, I looked to Grindr as the gay man's path to marriage. Being queer on Capitol Hill felt more like the rule rather than the exception. The Hill was an anomaly I had never experienced before. My coworker had worked as a go-go dancer, or maybe he was a bartender, at a nightclub called R Place. Throughout our short friendship, he had become the confidant who subtly yet unknowingly eased me out of discipleship and into the "real world."

A year before leaving the ICOC, I invited him to church. I hoped to baptize him. He politely declined. Instead, he extended an invitation to hang out at a small get-together at a house near the University of Washington. I reluctantly agreed because I wanted a reason to be around him. I mostly had a giant crush on the guy, but I also believed it was my duty to save his soul. Who is to say the two worlds couldn't collide?

"Is it fun? You know... going to the gay bars?" I asked him, deep-throating a hint of reservation.

"Yeah! R place is a lot of fun! Lots of cute boys and strong drinks!"

When King County Gymnastics went on its annual holiday break a few months later, I took the opportunity to visit my parents in Spokane. I stood on the brink of abandoning my faith but struggled to pull the trigger. Several hours before my departure at the Greyhound Station, I walked three miles in the frigid weather. Walking under an overpass, I saw homeless folks standing around, fires burning in metal trash cans; beyond the overpass, a church contrasted against the backdrop of skyscrapers and bustling traffic beside me. There might have even been snow on the ground, I don't remember, but the cold felt biting.

My mission that night was to catch a glimpse of Capitol Hill and what life would be like apart from my adherence to the ICOC. I wanted to circle R Place to feel the vibe out. Would I have the courage to go inside? Walking along Pine Street across from Walgreens, I noticed R Place in the distance. It was a Friday night, with drunk people stumbling about, girls and gays inextricably linked together, laughing, and some puking on the road in front of their Uber. I could see the dark, dingy-looking four-story building shrouded in green neon lights.

(Cue I Know Places (Taylor's Version) by Taylor Swift)

Posters hung outside the club showing men in thongs advertising various bar-sponsored events and daily drink specials. I felt like I was walking in slow motion. I couldn't tell if I felt excited or nauseous. I wanted to be in the club, but at the same time, I wanted nothing to do with it. I was a committed follower of Jesus Christ—not some active homosexual who gave in willy-nilly to the lure of hot men in speedos or gray sweatpants. I held myself to a higher standard than this bar could offer me. Still, I glanced at another sign advertising *Robbie Turner's Playground* as a line formed at the entrance to the club. A few hot guys caught my attention before I continued past the club, leaving me to wonder what could have been had I ventured inside.

I was at the small get-together when I looked at my phone—an hour had passed. My coworker held a bottle at me. "Want a beer?"

I waved my hand, "Oh, no thank you. I don't drink."

"You sure man?"

"I'm good, thanks, though!"

"Alright." He shrugged it off, popped the cap, then took a swig. I wondered if I might be in sin. The environment felt uncomfortably relaxed. Everything felt dirty: the house, the people, and the energy. The whole atmosphere needed spiritual cleansing. I tried to channel my inner faith, hoping the Holy Spirit would step in and guide me as all my disciple's had taught me. I longed to be back at the church fellowshipping with disciples.

My escape from the church filled me with regrets, and they flew at me with ferocity. It was sickening. I lamented the effort I spent suppressing my sexuality. I cringed at the conversations I engaged with my former teammates and coworkers. I tried selling a smoke screen of peace and contentment. Now, a deep hatred for Christianity had replaced my zeal. Why would God allow me to carry the burden of a sexuality I never chose? Why did God create me fully knowing I'd burn in Hell simply because I couldn't handle the rules? Did God express his love in this way? I needed a distraction from the noise. I wanted to embark on a path to self-acceptance, but I didn't know where to start.

One afternoon after my shift ended at King County Gymnastics, I participated in Open Gym (free play for coaches). Several months had passed since I practiced gymnastics, and I wanted to see if I could pick up where I left off. Besides my shoddy endurance, I could still tumble proficiently. Flipping around the gym, however, still brought me immense joy, a feeling I had forgotten. I sat at the edge of the tumble track, thinking about how comical my situation was. ICOC leaders always preached joy as the byproduct of personal commitment to Jesus. Yet, I only experienced the opposite. Joy was having freedom from legalistic church rules.

Adam Whitaker stood in the distance, chatting with coaches gently bouncing on the trampoline. Whitaker was the head Trampoline and Tumbling coach at the club. Getting Whitaker's attention was my ticket back to gymnastics. I began tumbling on the tumble track because I wanted him to see what I could do as a gymnast. This opportunity felt reminiscent of when I attended the U.S. Elite Challenge in Spokane a few years prior. Trampoline and Tumbling (T&T) came back full circle. I hoped for an uncomplicated return to the sport. I needed to impress Whitaker, and I needed to do it quickly. I ran into a round-off handspring double-back tuck, hoping to get a second look. My timing was perfect.

"Woah there, kid! Nice double back tuck!" Whitaker yelled in my direction.

"Thanks!" I yelled back. I approached him. "I heard you coach the Trampoline and Tumbling team here! What's it like? Is it fun?" I already knew the answer. I wanted Whitaker to roll out the red carpet for me to waltz onto the team.

"Yeah man, it's great. The kids are great. I have another athlete joining this summer who is about your age, too."

"Would you mind if I trained with you guys this summer, too?"

"Let me give you my email and we can chat further about getting you to coach some T&T classes here in addition to training."

I got on board with this plan. Training as a collegiate gymnast might have been off the table, but training club gymnastics was not. Could I still become an elite gymnast?

Obsessively swiping Tinder was my new hobby. I'd swipe, match with guys, and chat for a bit. Days later, I'd ghost them, or they'd ghost me. I felt insecure and unsure of how to navigate the LGBTQ community. All the men on Tinder and Grindr seemed confident and sure of themselves. I sat on bus number 44, taking me from Ballard to the University District, swiping when I noticed a photo of my teammate, Julian. Julian had black hair and pale white skin and looked incredibly buff. I would have never suspected him as gay or, at least, bisexual. He was handsome, but the situation felt like a trap. Was I supposed to swipe left? Swipe right? What if we matched? I felt conflicted with the situation.

We'd regularly see each other in the gym, and I didn't want to come on too strong. I closed Tinder to refresh the app to continue swiping while I thought about it more.

Left, Left, Left, Right, Julian 23.

When his photo reappeared, I took a deep breath and swiped right. *It's a Match!* A toggle prompting me to send him a message popped up on my screen. Feelings were mutual. I had only been on the T&T team for two days when this happened, and Julian and I had only interacted once as partners for a conditioning assignment. Did Julian realize his most recent match was also his teammate? I wasn't sure and felt nervous to point it out, even if it was blatantly obvious.

The Fiasco

Charles finally kicked me out. I had overstayed my tenancy when I dropped out of Seattle Central Community College. I had become wholly unwelcome at his house once I ceased my devotion to the ICOC. Charles grabbed his computer and sat on a couch before a coffee table. "You have one week to find another place to live, Kenny. Let's get to looking on Craigslist. I'll even help you out." He opened his MacBook and put his glasses on to scour the housing section. We spent an hour browsing when finally we got an answer about a single-bedroom occupancy. The room would be in a shared house in the Lake City area, only fifteen minutes from King County Gymnastics. After several back-and-forth messages, the landlord offered me a same-day property tour. The Craigslist ad advertised rent at only five hundred dollars, so I jumped at the opportunity because I needed somewhere else to live as quickly as possible.

The homeowner looked like a character I would have expected from a horror movie. He was a skeletal figure, missing a finger, sporting overalls, no shirt, and a thick blanket of back and shoulder hair. Patches of thin, long, scraggly hair fell from his head, and his sideburns connected into similarly awkward patches of white chin hair. He also boasted, proudly, several missing teeth. I felt like I was staring down a mix between Otis B. Driftwood and one of those backwoods-hillbilly cannibals from the Wrong Turn franchise.

"Do you live here, too?" I asked, trying to sound casual. I wasn't about to live under the same roof as this man.

"No! I don't..."

"Oh, praise God!" I blurted before I realized what I said. I quickly added, "that your garage door is in working order. Where I currently live, I have to lift and close it manually."

"Ope. Yep, just bought a replacement. I accidentally crashed my van through the original door."

You what?

The house was old—a creaky hardwood floor in the living room and various colored shag carpets throughout the bedrooms. The place looked retrofitted in the 1970s. My bedroom, which included orange shag, had the bottom portion of the walls covered in shiplap; the upper half of the wall painted a forest green. The bedroom came complete with a deadbolt lock, cheap enough to budget with my work schedule. The roommates were all young professionals. The house was empty and quiet upon my inspection. I figured I had nothing to worry about, so I wasted no time signing the lease because I had to leave for work.

I was unpacking my belongings in the middle of my bedroom floor. I hung my shirts in the closet and lined my books along the edge of my window sill. There was a knock at my door. "Hey, new guy!" a girl's voice wafted through the door. When I opened it,

I saw she had bleached blond hair with pink highlights, holding onto clear boxing tape.

"What's up?" I asked.

She walked away toward the living room. "You know this place has bedbugs, right?"

I followed her out, "I beg your pardon?" I watched as she wrapped a box of her belongings in plastic wrap.

"I thought you might not know. Just look around!" She pulled the tape around the box, sealing it completely. "I'm breaking my lease."

"Are you serious?" I made a cursory glance around the living room.

"I'm afraid so. The trim of the floor is permanently crusted with these little fuckers!"

I felt lightheaded. This girl temporarily kept me grounded. She seemed edgy and cool, most likely an artist. She told me she had signed her lease three days earlier and discovered the infestation in passing through the previous tenant who occupied my unit before me. That guy had also moved out in a hurry.

The following day, I called the landlord. "Why did you neglect to inform me about the BED BUG infestation in the house?"

He spoke with a distinct southern draw I didn't remember him having before. "Oh, some of the guys did complain about this a few years ago."

"You've done nothing to address this for years?"

"I thought you knew. Let me get ya some bug spray! That should do the trick!"

"No, it shouldn't! You need to call an exterminator! I'm moving out!"

"Okay, okay, okay, hold yer horses. Let me see if I can find someone to take yer place."

I was broke and didn't have another place lined up. I paid what little I had saved to get into this bedroom. I spent the rest of the afternoon pacing back and forth. What if the landlord doesn't give me my money back? What if I become homeless? I caught the bus downtown to Target and bought a cheap camping tent. When I got home, I built it on the bedroom floor. If I did become homeless, at least I'd have a tent.

The landlord phoned me the following day. Good news. Sort of. "I found ya someone to take yer bedroom. But I will only give you half yer rent back."

"Your house is infested with bed bugs! I need the full amount back!"

"Oh, don't be ridiculous. No, it's not."

"Yes! It is! You've had three people break their lease because of it."

"I'm not the idiot who signed a lease broke it off a day later, am I?"

That was our final conversation. The landlord cut me a check for less than half of what I paid him. I would have immediately been homeless on the streets of Seattle if it weren't for two disciples who lived just outside of city limits. They didn't hesitate to let me move into their home in Auburn, WA. Hours later, I trashed what I couldn't salvage and took my clothes to a laundry mat to cook whatever bugs might have climbed into my wardrobe. I later discovered that the person who replaced me broke their lease shortly after.

Returning to gymnastics was sudden and intense, especially after my move to Auburn. In the morning, I taught classes at King County Gymnastics near Lake City, about 34 miles north of where I lived. I didn't have a car, so I made the commute all over Seattle by metro. In the afternoons, I caught the bus to the gym's second location near Ballard for a second shift of classes, followed by practice with Julian under Whitaker's direction. The daily commute into Seattle from Auburn left me with no wiggle room. I was on a bus or in a gym. I left the apartment at 5:00 a.m. and returned around 11:00 p.m. I had to catch five buses daily to make the situation work; I tried to make the most of unfavorable circumstances. Training gymnastics again, however, made it feel worthwhile. I told myself the chaos couldn't last forever and that my circumstances would get better in the future.

Furthermore, doing gymnastics with my Tinder match sounded to me like a match made in heaven—something almost too perfect. The problem was I couldn't give him the time of day because I needed to be at all my bus stops on time; otherwise, I might not make it home for the evening. I felt like Cinderella trying to coordinate a time to hang out.

Auburn, WA, immediately took its toll on me. One morning, I missed my connecting bus into downtown Seattle. I rushed off the bus and immediately called an Uber, costing me sixty-eight dollars. I didn't have the money to spare for a ride to work. I worked minimum wage. Despite my effort and shelling out cash, I didn't have, I still arrived late to work as my Uber hit the morning traffic rush. I lamented in my journal:

Does God hate me? What did I do to deserve such a hopeless, miserable life? I can't afford it. It's not fair. I work hard every day. I'm doing my best, but my best isn't enough.

I needed an act of God. Thankfully, a reprieve came to me as a Facebook post from a disciple named Joshua.

Hi Facebook,

We're looking for a fourth male roommate for our apartment in the University District area.

I sent Joshua a message expressing my readiness to move in immediately. I should have considered the type of household I'd be living in. But I didn't because the University District was a stone's throw away from Lake City, Ballard, and Capitol Hill. The living situation would be with a group of campus disciples who didn't know me well. Did Joshua realize I was no longer a church member? Did he read my post about no longer living as a disciple? I don't think he did. I took advantage of the situation by moving in on the pretense that I still attended church. Any other living arrangement would have sufficed, especially since I wanted to rebrand myself. But desperate times called for desperate measures, I told myself. I needed to find suitable housing; from the looks of it, the three campus disciples needed someone to fill a fourth spot immediately.

A few weeks later, in late Fall 2015, I moved into apartment number 28, a two-bed, two-bath unit at the Wingate Apartments in the University District. The apartment sat right behind Greek Row. I saw my current living situation as a toxic cosmic pairing. Perhaps some twisted joke on God's part. Who knows?

I didn't fully disclose my status as a fallaway from the church until after I had signed the lease. My new roommates unexpectedly supported my decision to no longer be a church member (as much as they could). Their supportive positions were to show kindness and bring me to repentance (they wanted to take me back to church). I was well-rehearsed in their tango and fluent in their jargon. I only moved in because I wanted cheap rent and proximity to Ballard, Lake City, and Capitol Hill.

The debris had settled from the aftershock of my abrupt exit from the ICOC and the wild housing situations over the last few months. I felt like I could finally breathe. I could get on track to begin saving money. I'd coach classes, train under Whitaker, and perhaps even form a relationship with Julian. Everything would be sailing smoothly from here on out. Additionally, I could now afford minor luxuries like Starbucks and weekend excursions not involving evangelism.

Training under Whitaker through the Summer and Fall, I had progressed better than anticipated; I could now throw a full-twisting double backflip on the floor with relative ease. I trained double layouts on the tumble track and worked drills to prepare me for a full-out. A full-out is a preface skill to the full-full, otherwise known as a double-twisting double backflip (two flips; two twists—one skill). I had Julian to keep me mentally focused on being an upgraded version of myself in the gym. Even better, I could spend time with him after practice hours.

Julian and I had tentative plans to meet at R Place. However, he didn't know if he could make it. It had something to do with his ex-boyfriend and petty drama. Fair enough. I caught bus number 49 to Capitol Hill and walked to R Place. I hadn't rehearsed for my grand entrance into the gay bar. I had no clue how to function in an LGBTQ environment. I felt uneasy yet excited. I stood outside studying the nightclub for several minutes to see which doors patrons used to enter before finally mustering the courage to walk in through the side door. Inside, R Place seemed like a quaint bar.

Only a handful of people sat around the bar, chatting and drinking while the U.S. top ten music videos played on the TV screens above the bar. As soon as I sat down, the bartender caught my eye and came over to greet me as quickly as I entered. "Can I take a quick peek at your ID?"

Fuck.

I handed the bartender my ID. I wasn't ready for immediate attention.

"How's it going? What can I get started for you?"

"Uh," I hesitated. "I don't know. I've never done this before."

I viewed myself as a loser; I assumed he must have seen me the same. The bartender stood tall, muscular, and incredibly handsome. He had an animated personality and enlivened the bar with his presence. Everyone seemed to like him. He made an effort to make me feel at home by asking about my preferences in taste. "So," he leaned over the bar. "Are you into sweet or sour?"

"Uh sweet, I think. Something fun I guess."

Minutes later, he returned. "Here you go. Tell me what you think!"

I took a sip of the fruity concoction. "It's good! What's it called?"

"Sex on the Beach!"

After a half hour of nursing the cocktail, a warm fuzzy feeling enveloped my forehead and legs. I sat on a stool, swinging my legs back and forth, hoping Julian would arrive any moment. Suddenly, three gay men surrounded me.

"Can I sit here?" one of them asked me.

"Sure," I said, looking straight ahead.

"And what is your name?"

"Kenny," I said, attempting to mask my discomfort.

The first guy reminded me of George Michael; he introduced himself as Carly. Then rehearsed anecdotes from his childhood before veering into a story about a guy he slept with named Kenny and how he did gymnastics and could sit in all sorts of wild positions while fucking. I didn't know how to respond to the story. Did I mention to Carly that I did gymnastics? I felt disconnected and kept my responses short.

"Uh huh."

"Ohhhh."

"Okay cool!"

My interactions in the bar were not comfortable. I didn't know how to interact with a bunch of flagrant homosexuals. I didn't know how to stop viewing them through the lenses of my discipleship. I felt out of place, but the buzz from the alcohol helped me relax into the scene. Still, I hoped now more than ever that Julian would walk through the door so I'd have a reason to exit the conversation.

After my second sex on the beach, I felt more blunt. "So let me get this straight. You're a boy whose name is Carly?"

Carly giggled. "Oh sweetheart! You must be new here. Gender is a social construct and my pronouns are she/they."

"How does that work?"

Carly's friend tapped me on the shoulder, acrylic nails ready to kill. "Hunty, listen. This is Carly, SHE is a legend in Seattle. This is Carly, THEY are nonbinary. Got it?"

"In this community, we never assume gender," the third friend, wearing a red and orange caftan, said. It felt like a script from Mean Girls, and I was Lindsey Lohan's character.

"Don't be mean Candra," Carly said, "This fella is still wet behind the ears; his umbilical cord is practically still attached."

Candra pointed their bright pink nails toward me. "Carly! Did you assume his gender?"

"You are a boy, are you not?" Carly asked in the same way a principal might reprimand a student.

I pulled my head back. "Uh, Yeah?"

Carly waved their hand. "Sis. See? He said it himself."

I excused myself to order another cocktail and explore the bar more—still no sign of Julian. I sent him a text message.

> Are you coming out tonight?

"Dahling," Candra called out to me as I stood waiting for my next sex on the beach. "Everyone will be dancing on the third floor later this evening. Go upstairs and find yourself a cute man for the evening."

"Noted." I grabbed my drink and climbed the second-floor stairs to explore. The third floor was opening up as I got to the second floor. I kicked back several more cocktails the rest of the night and found the courage to dance on the main stage. One guy messaged me on Grindr to call me a firecracker on the dance floor. At the night's end, the lights illuminated the dance floor—closing time. Who knew a night out could go by so quickly? I descended the stairs in a cluster of sweaty bodies.

"Keep moving! Keep moving! Keep moving!" One of R Place's main bouncers yelled from the bottom of the staircase. She was friendly and personable but didn't mess around regarding her job. She was almost like a mother to the community. She helped see me out the side door with everyone else.

Once I got outside, I realized Julian never came out. He didn't even bother to text me back. I caught an Uber back at the Wingate around 2:30 in the morning, hammered. My roommates were in the middle of an intense bible study with a guy interested in being baptized into the church. His name was Gabe, and he played baseball for the University of Washington. We had met only once before, during one of my panic visits to church. The conflict between my sexuality and faith often coerced me to attend worship on Sundays. My visits were usually an attempt to calm my nerves.

"Ayyy Carlo!" I stumbled into the coffee table.

"Carlo? Name's Gabe, bro, remember? You drunk?"

I giggled at the mistake but continued using his undesired pseudonym. "Carlo! Listen, Carlo," I slurred my speech, "I am so drunk right now!"

Joshua stood from the couch and helped get me to my feet. "Kenny, man, let's get you some water and take you to bed! How does that sound?"

"Bitch, I only drink vodka now!"

"I know you do," he said understandingly, "but here's some water now, too! Let's get you to bed. Okay?"

"You're a good guy." I leaned into him for stability.

"Thank you, Kenny. Let's get you tucked into bed."

"I am so drunk... You're mad at me huh? God's mad at me, too."

"I know you are, bud. But I'm not mad at you and neither is God."

"Goodnight Joshua."

"Goodnight, bud."

Joshua was a class act. He was the type of person who had a knack for genuine empathy.

The Friday before Thanksgiving, around 11:00 p.m., I unexpectedly ran into Julian at R Place. I was drinking alone on the second floor when he appeared from the staircase and walked toward me.

"Hey!" I called out to him.

"Oh. Hey."

We stood awkwardly for several minutes; I took a selfie with him. My exchanges with Julian were proving odd. Was he always this devoid of color? He had no personality. Boyfriend material, I must have thought. Was he attracted to me still? I asked him if he still wanted to go out on a date, cross-referencing our Tinder match several weeks earlier. He said he did. What I remember next about our time together is a montage of booze and running around Capitol Hill. I know we danced together at R Place a few times, his cocktail spilling everywhere as he swayed like a tree. He also invited me to his living quarters—a bedroom in a flying Trapeze Warehouse in the SODO neighborhood. I didn't find it odd, though. He wanted to be in Cirque du Soleil.

"You can't let anyone know I let you in here after hours. We're not supposed to have guests here." Julian said as he invited me to climb the ladder, lay in the trapeze net, and hold hands.

His bedroom was along the outer edge of the building. Did we have sex that night? I know he had to teach a recreational circus class the following day. I also became acquainted with some flying trapeze artists living in the warehouse. When I woke up in the morning, I had to sneak out of the building to avoid the company's owners seeing me come out of Julian's bedroom. Later that same day, after Julian finished work, we wandered past the Starbucks Reserve Roastery on our way to the Seattle Eagle.

He opened the door to the bar. "A lot of guys who want me are going to hate you because we are hanging out."

One of those guys was Julian's ex-boyfriend, who discovered he had turned his detached affection toward me. I had suddenly become public enemy number one. I didn't realize he was entertaining his ex and stringing me along. I didn't know until I was drunk in his arms, waltzing into his spiteful exes' apartment for an unplanned meet and greet. How did I get in this position? What on earth was happening?

As soon as we walked through the door, his severely intoxicated ex ripped Julian away from me. "See Kenny. HE'S MINE," he said, slurring his speech.

They started making out. Julian's ex helped him pull his shirt off, and then he got on his knees, attempting to pull his pants off as if I wasn't even there, like a scene from a terrible X-rated rom-com. Did Julian understand what was happening? They both seemed hopelessly high and intoxicated, but I figured he must have known. I slipped out of the apartment and changed his contact info on my phone to Fruit Cake. That'll teach him.

The Fiasco Continues

As autumn turned to winter, I tapered into the daily grind of coaching more than training. King County Gymnastics only allotted Julian and me one hour to tumble with the T&T team a few nights per week. Afterward, we jumped right back into coaching. Julian taught the pre-team, the group of kids who would soon compete. I got stuck teaching a boy's recreational T&T class—or, how I viewed it—glorified babysitting. I hated these kids, and for the most part, these kids hated me back. Whitaker liked them and wanted to pull three or four of them onto the pre-team next season. They were rowdy and had no sense of structure. I spent the hour frustrated at how rambunctious they acted. "Boys!" I'd furiously shout, "Stop climbing on this mat when you return to the tumble track!"

As predicted, they ignored my barking. They found it hilarious. I can't blame them, though. I would have acted the same. While tumbling, James would do a cartwheel, then follow it up with a booty pop, snapping his fingers above his head. It made me giggle, but the move didn't seem appropriate for class, so I told him to stop. Ivan hated me because I often yelled at him for goofing around with James. He also didn't hide the fact he hated me.

"I hate you so much, coach Kenny. I think you're the stupidest coach in the whole entire world!" He said to me as class ended.

"Well, I like you a lot and think you're the BEST kid in the world!" I retorted sarcastically.

Whitaker jumped into the commotion, unbothered by Ivan's disdain for me. "What's his problem?"

"I don't know. He doesn't like me."

"Uh... Okay. Anyway," he proceeded, "listen, we have our first travel meet of the season in January, so you'll want to start thinking about your hotel and airfare for the meet in Dyer, Indiana. You'll want to fly into Chicago O'Hare airport, and I can come get you from there."

I wanted to avoid traveling to compete since I would only be eligible to compete as a level 9. "Could I wait to travel once I hit mobility to compete level 10 or elite?"

Whitaker looked at me incredulously. "No, you can't. If you're a part of my team, you'll travel to every competition to compete. Plus, I'll need you on the floor as a coach."

Shouldn't the gym pay for my hotel and airfare if Whitaker needed me on the floor to coach? Why didn't he previously inform me about all the travel meets? Did he realize my salary wasn't enough to cover all the travel expenses? Thanks to the tabs I accrued at R Place nightly and the lease I had signed at the Wingate Apartments, I had already fallen a couple hundred dollars in debt. I relied entirely on my credit card for daily expenses like food, coffee, and an ORCA bus pass. Since the competition wasn't until February, I booked through Expedia, thinking it would be the cheaper option—I'd seen the commercials before. I told myself I would pay it back later.

I began to notice a glaring disparity between Julian and me. Whitaker treated him like the shining star of the T&T program, both as an athlete and a coach. I frequently compared myself to him. Once, Whitaker approached me, preparing for a vacation. "Julian is in charge when I'm gone. Whatever he says is absolute gospel!"

Was I supposed to be Julian's subordinate for the week while Whitaker drank margaritas and snorkeled in the ocean? Working in Julian's shadow only fueled my disdain for him and, more recently, the gymnastics industry.

The night before my first-ever gymnastics meet, I had a productive practice until the end. I heard a loud *crunch* in my ear. My right leg slipped out of my hand mid-double backflip during my last tumbling pass, and I landed on one foot. I imagine I looked like an ill-spiraling football thrown by a six-year-old. Whitaker walked over to me.

"Oh, it doesn't look bad! You'll be fine for tomorrow." He chirped.

I was on my back, pulling my leg in. "No Whitaker, it's broken!"

"Nah! You'll be good as new tomorrow!"

I writhed on the floor. "Fuck! Fuck! Fuck! This shit hurts so bad!"

"Oh... Maybe you're not fine!"

The pain was excruciating. Whitaker called Julian to assist. I hoped he'd come to comfort me like a boyfriend. Instead, he brought me a bucket of ice water to stick my ankle in and coldly walked away. One of my student's parents drove me to the University Medical Center to get fitted for a cast and crutches. I arrived at work the following Monday because nobody could cover my preschool classes on such short notice. I hobbled through the gym lobby on crutches. Whitaker shook his head, walking away into the manager's office. Whitaker knew I couldn't teach the class; some of the group's four-year-olds often bolted away. I had asked Julian to cover my shift the night before, but he said no. He agreed, however, once Whitaker told him to cover my classes.

I watched Julian in the background, setting up obstacle courses for the preschool classes he would now teach. I looked at Whitaker. "Do you think I'll get a refund for my plane ticket to Chicago?"

Whitaker clicked his pen repeatedly, "What airline did you book through?"

"I didn't go through an airline? I booked through Expedia."

"There's your mistake." The clicking stopped. "Never book through a third party. Always purchase directly through the airline. I doubt you'll get a refund on your ticket."

I dwelled on the fact I had wasted extra money I didn't have. I wasn't flying into Chicago to compete. While chewing over this news, the front desk registrar called my name as Whitaker walked away.

"Hey Kenny," she said, "when you have a free moment, can you come and take care of your comp fee?"

I pulled my head back, raising an eyebrow, "Comp fee?"

"Yes, it looks like you have additional expenses from November through April."

"Oh, well how much do I owe?"

"Three-hundred-seventy-eight dollars a month."

I grew wide-eyed and gasped. "Though April?"

She turned her computer screen toward me. "That's what it looks like."

"Oh, okay..." I fumbled for my credit card.

Why were all the vast expenses plaguing me? Why did I have to deal with all these roadblocks? I didn't make enough to cover the additional costs and felt too scared to address the situation directly. I felt fearful to admit I had unwittingly bitten off a more significant chunk than I could chew. I later discovered the comp fees covered Julian and Whitaker's airfare and hotel expenses at all the travel meets and a per diem check for the weekend. I didn't get such a luxury. Whitaker seemed to expect me to pay for everything on my own. Did he think I had limitless finances? I didn't understand why Julian received preferential treatment. I had coached at King County Gymnastics for two years before he showed up.

Additionally, I discovered that Julian made nearly two times my hourly rate. Was his contribution to the gym worth that much more than mine? I assumed Whitaker wanted Julian to compete as an elite-level power tumbler, so he helped streamline the process by rolling out the red carpet at the gym's expense. To say I felt jealous is an understatement. I practically foamed at the mouth, livid. With a looming hospital bill and ongoing competition fees despite the injury not allowing me to compete, even more devastating news awaited me at the Wingate.

I was lying down and elevating my foot. From the corner of my eye, I noticed a little bug crawling along the crease of the futon. I had seen one before but didn't initially connect the dots. Now the little bugger was staring me down. I hopped on one foot out of the bedroom. "Houston, we have a problem!"

The boys looked up at me. "What is it?"

"We have bedbugs!"

"What!" Joshua said, "No, we don't!"

"If you don't believe me, come check it out!"

The boys all ran into our bedroom to examine the futon.

"There! See!" I pointed. The bugs marched along the crease of the couch, leading to a pile of laundry.

"Go check your rooms and your beds!" Joshua commanded. Everyone dispersed like cockroaches to their bedrooms, only to report no bed bugs. The bugs were only in our room. How could this have happened? Did I accidentally bring them with me? Almost immediately, the accusations came rolling in.

"Kenny, they had to have come from you," one of the roommates said, looking at me, "you're the only one who dealt with this exact situation, and they're in your room and your room only!"

"I did not, you guys. I threw all my belongings away and took my clothes to the laundromat."

"Joshua!" I pointed at him to take the attention off me. "You brought them back to our apartment!"

Joshua had recently taken a trip with his family to the Bahamas. Some of his vacation luggage lay where the infestation seemed contained. Joshua admitted as much. "Oh shoot, you're probably right. I am so sorry, guys! We will get this figured out with the landlord."

In the meantime, we sprayed copious amounts of bug spray around the apartment, including our second-floor hallway leading into the shared laundry room. Soon, reports of bedbugs infesting neighboring apartments began circulating. The neighbor directly below us experienced them. We discovered the real culprit of this infestation through our landlord. It wasn't Joshua. It was the apartment directly above ours. From what I heard, the apartment infestation was so horrific that they evicted the tenants and had to do floor-to-ceiling renovations on the unit. During that time, the only washing machine on our floor stopped working, so the entire second floor had to use either the first- or third-floor washer and dryer. Joshua and I used the third-floor laundry room numerous times, so we likely tracked the bugs into our apartment through our trips upstairs. The apartment complex hired an exterminator to spray each apartment individually over two weeks.

I hyper-fixated on getting drunk at R Place after work. Getting shitfaced nightly was my favorite activity. As my body metabolized the alcohol, I could easily separate from who I was deep down. I felt overjoyed to have the LGBTQ version of the Holy Spirit (multiple shots of vodka) guiding my frontal lobe. Thus, a routine in my life emerged: Work, practice, shower, R Place, then stumble home fucked up beyond all recognition. Then, I'd nurse my hangover the next afternoon in preparation to do it all over again.

Julian and I eventually made amends somewhere in the timeline (I don't always learn from my mistakes the first time around). We started hanging out again. We got a hotel for a weekend downtown, drank cheap wine, and cuddled all night. He had finally gotten rid of the toxic ex once and for all, he said. I danced around to the news. Still, I wanted to know what the parameters of our relationship were. Fuck buddies? Boyfriends? A hybrid mix? Later in the competitive season, Julian qualified for an Elite Qualifier called the U.S. Elite Challenge. King County Gymnastics flew Whitaker and Julian to the U.S. Olympic Training Center in Colorado Springs for the competition. I felt jealous that I couldn't go, but I was excited for my new *whatever-we-were*. The following week, I noticed Julian didn't attend practice; I asked about his whereabouts.

Whitaker threw his hands up. "I don't know, and I don't care at the moment! He quit!"

He what?

Push came to shove while they were away. Whitaker and Julian got into a petty argument over something, and Julian never got onto his return flight back to Seattle at the end of the competition. Did this mark the end of our *whatever-we-were?* I texted him, but he ghosted me. I changed his contact info back to Fruit Cake—the name it remains to this day. I had long forgotten about these incidents until recently, browsing through my journals from 2015 and 2016.

Several weeks after the exterminators did their rounds, the bedbugs returned full force to the apartment complex with a vengeance. It was around the last month of our lease. The end of the Wingate brother's household slowly crept up. The other brothers made plans to join new households somewhere else. The circumstances at the Wingate were too challenging to manage. It wasn't just the bedbugs. I was a problematic roommate to live with. During my time living at the unit, I was a nuisance. I constantly arrived home in the middle of the night drunk, disregarded the house rules, was tremendously unhelpful and messy, and made a concerted effort to be an asshole, sometimes even mocking their faith.

Joshua got married, and if I remember correctly, he signed a lease for him and his wife—a one-bedroom at the Wingate (he signed it before discovering the bedbugs had returned). After Joshua moved down the hall from apartment 28, I had our shared bedroom all to myself. The apartment complex had exterminators go from apartment to apartment for treatment again. But not too long after the second round of extermination, Joshua said the bedbugs had returned a third time. His apartment had now become infested. There seemed no escape. Then somebody burglarized the complex's mailbox. They broke in and threw everyone's mail across the bottom of the staircase. Residents were jumping ship, moving out left and right; they threw bug-infested furniture out of windows into the alley below. I wanted to leave, too, but kept turning up empty-handed in my search for affordable housing because I didn't have the money to do so.

One by one, the other three brothers began leaving for their new living situations. During the final week of our lease, they all came to help clear out the unit. One of the brothers and I stood in my bedroom while Joshua waited outside in the alley below the window to my bedroom.

The brother next to me yelled out the window, "is the coast clear?" as we lined the edge of the futon to the window sill.

"Yeah!" Joshua echoed back up.

"Alright, we're in the clear. Ready?"

"Ready!"

"3-2-1 and push!"

We began pushing the futon.

"Stop! Stop! Stop!"

"Did he say stop?" the brother next to me asked. "What?" he yelled out as the futon stuck halfway out the window.

"Okay! The car passed! You can push it out all the way now!"

"Alrighty then," He looked at me. "3-2-1 and push!"

Crack! Bang! The furniture echoed below as it hit the pavement.

The futon was one of several items we pushed out of the bedroom window. We had a blast doing the work. It added a fun secondary purpose to moving. I lived at the Wingate alone for the remainder of the lease, wondering where I would go next. I still needed to secure somewhere else to live. After they left to settle into their new apartments, I scoured every available Craigslist ad, hoping for a lead. When nothing came about, I sat in the empty apartment, contemplating my life. The future never felt so uncertain. I hated how expensive it was to exist in the world. Life was hard, but I would make it work.

The Hobbit Hole and Throne Room

The new girl at King County Gymnastics walked through the lobby loud and rambunctiously. I wondered all day who she was as she strolled about the gym, making friendly conversation with a group of four-year-old girls and the coach she shadowed for the day. Her personality seemed bubbly and silly, yet mysterious. Her look didn't fit the description of a girl who could relate to preschool-aged children. She looked vampiric but carried a sense of humor, causing the children to burst into maniacal cackles. The moment she walked through the door into the coach's office, a shift in the energy took place. Everyone's curiosity centered on her.

"Listen bitch!" I called out to her with my best gay accent, "We need to be Facebook friends!"

Jackie McCartin had moved to Seattle from Southern California on a full-ride scholarship to compete in gymnastics at the University of Washington. A former elite-level gymnast, she spent her gymnastics career at a prominent club in the West Covina area. She was the only elite-level gymnast I had encountered in real life. It felt like a dream come true, actively engaging in friendship with someone who got to live my fantasy as an actual YouTube gymnast. Was this reality? Did I have what it took to become friends with someone like her? Her gymnastics career must have been part of the conversation because I can't remember everything we discussed. Within a few minutes of our initial interaction, Jack invited me, or perhaps I took it upon myself, to join a party inside her shirt. We were suddenly like conjoined twins sharing her staff shirt. The connection was instantaneous and unforgettable. Her overall vibe and demeanor drew me close; I had never met someone I felt I could be so unashamedly loud and weird around. She was confident and monolithically occupied space in every social situation.

The day before I met Jack, I sat against the closet mirror blankly, picking at the floor dandruff, contemplating life. Save for the twin-size mattress once belonging to Joshua and a few of my items, the brothers had all vacated, and I only had three days to follow suit. I cringed at how disheveled the cream-colored carpet had become. Would the apartment complex return our security deposit? Would we be on the hook for damages? It wouldn't have surprised me in the condition we left the apartment. I felt truly alone in this moment. Unlike my former roommates, I didn't have parents I could financially rely on to get me through difficult transitions like this. Their parents had cut them checks for rent and even bought them cars and nice ones, too. Some took random vacations to places like Puerto Vallarta, the Bahamas, or even Europe. Their parents could afford to put them through college. I had a pity party. Perhaps it was a pity party I thought I had earned. I didn't feel like I had anything to be grateful for. I could only focus on what I didn't have instead of what I did.

In the coach's office, I mentioned my search for a bedroom. Jack looked at me and said, "Oh, my roommate moved out a few weeks ago! If you need a space, I have an opening."

I thanked God. I could only view this as an act from above. Surprisingly, we also got our security deposit back from the Wingate. My portion only amounted to three hundred or so dollars, enough to contribute to the security deposit at Jack's. I moved into her house the next night.

The Hobbit Hole and Throne Room, located in the University District at 4724 7th Ave NE, only a few blocks from the Wingate, is a fitting name for the basement converted apartment I had settled into. The front door sat inelegantly in a hole, like an egress window. The ceiling tilted dramatically, giving the illusion of a fun house.

"Did you ever notice how the ceiling tilts?" I asked one day.

Jack looked at the ceiling curiously and walked into the kitchen. "No, I haven't." Her fingers touched the ceiling as she walked from the kitchen into the living room until her fingertips could no longer touch by a couple of feet. "Woah!" She giggled. "How the fuck have I never noticed this before?"

The Bathroom looked equally bizarre, complete with a vaulted ceiling much taller than the rest of the apartment. The toilet sat like a throne on several irregularly shaped stairs, looking to the peasants below who might be showering. She dubbed it the Throne Room. Sometimes, the toilet would explode for no reason, and feces would fly everywhere. Afterward, the toilette would retch for several minutes as if hung over.

"Oh my god! Oh my god! Oh my god! The toilet is alive! It's breathing! It's alive right now! You could hear it dry heave before it vomited the excrement everywhere!" She announced through a Snapchat video. We spent a fair amount of time together creating and saving Snapchat videos—the backdrop of countless inside jokes.

I could not get over the fact that I could type Jack's name on YouTube and watch videos of her competing as a senior elite gymnast at competitions like the Visa Championships. However, her recollections of elite gymnastics didn't match my vision growing up. I became privy to a toxic and abusive culture within that side of the sport. Several months later, the USA Gymnastics Scandal broke. Hundreds of young women spanning several decades, all taken advantage of by The Deplorable, including Jack at the Visa Championships in 2010. She never took on a victim mindset, but the initial shock of repressed memories and emotions took a toll on her. When she returned as a coach, Jack knew who she wanted to be and what she wanted to give as a coach. "I would never treat kids the way my coaches treated me. I have hundreds of horror stories from my club career."

I looked at Jack, speechless. What was there to say? I didn't realize the world of elite gymnastics could be so cruel. She told me her story, "I was seven years old when a member of the 2000 Olympic Games trained at my gym. She was my idol, my hero growing up. I remember going to her every day while she worked out, and I'd tell her, 'I want to be like you when I grow up!' I'll always remember what she said to me. She said: 'No, you don't.' I never understood what she meant by it until after my elite career."

Jack only had negative reviews about her time at the Southern California Gymnastics Club. She talked about how one of her female coaches would dig her acrylic nails into her shoulders. She also spoke candidly about how her coaches routinely overtrained gymnasts to their satisfaction—maybe for their amusement. "They kept me at the bars until 11:00 p.m once. All because I didn't finish their assignment. I kept telling my coaches I physically couldn't do it because my hands were bloodied from rips. My coach's response to me was: 'Well, what are you going to do when you get to a meet, and you get a rip?'"

I sat there in silence, listening to her as she spoke. "I remember one time, my coach stopped the practice, lined everybody up, and had me stand before them. She said, 'Who here thinks Jackie deserves to attend Nationals this year? Raise your hand.' And, of course, nobody raised their hands because of fear. I don't blame them for complying. But what got me: after no one raised their hands, my coach continued berating me by saying 'See, not even your own teammates think you're worthy!'"

She seemed distant and nostalgic, reminiscing about her club career. Her coaches often taunted her, saying she was lazy and good for nothing. They'd tell her she didn't stack against elite gymnasts of her time and that trying was futile. The coaches at the Southern California Club had a knack for turning athletes against each other. Then, she competed on a broken ankle at the height of her club career. At the hospital, doctors confirmed Jack had broken her ankle, as suspected. Her coaches dismissed her and her parents, commenting: "Sorry your daughter is so fragile."

The author and Jack. Seattle Pride Fest. June 24th, 2018.

After moving in, Capitol Hill excursions became a nightly ritual. Though I physically broke free from the control of the church, I couldn't shake the indoctrination—it had firmly taken me captive.

Nightly cocktails at all the gay bars were the spike of assurance I needed to feel whole and alive. These spaces provided me with an identity and sense of belonging. I could arrive after work, rapidly guzzle several cocktails, settle into a brownout, and muster the courage to dance. I imagine I looked like a chameleon fresh out of the waters of homophobic ideology, sprinkled with social anxiety. Could people see me for who I was? Not that I wanted to be seen or spoken to unless I got sufficiently drunk. A dreadful doom occupied my attention most of the time. While sober, it slithered over me like a sandstorm. Alcohol took all the negative feelings away, and I'd feel normal. I'd feel joyful, even.

The bartenders at R Place cheerfully slung cocktails and poured cheap beers foaming over the glass, spilling into the well below the tap while patrons talked, laughed, and danced into the night. At the precise moment of a brownout, I felt like I belonged in the environment. The happy buzz never lasted long as I rapidly fell into a blackout. Once sufficiently plastered, I'd confess my love for one or all of the male bartenders and later wander upstairs to the club's third floor to dance. I continued drinking until I enthusiastically swapped saliva with the hot guy who kept giving me a *look* all night. I'd awaken early the following day, hungover, naked in his bed. The euphoria of sexual gratification could push negative feelings and proper decision-making to the wayside in the same manner alcohol could. I wanted to spend the rest of my life drinking or fucking.

Most nights, however, I'd catch an Uber back to the Hobbit Hole under the spell of a blackout, where I'd grace Jack with my alter ego, immortalized forever in Snapchat videos. On the second night living with her, I took an Uber home, entered her bedroom, and turned on the light.

"Oh. Are you sleeping?" I imagined myself saying to start the interruption.

Seeing me plastered, she hit the record button on her phone.

"Look what I can do," I said, bending forward to a ninety-degree angle and wiggling my shoulders while jumping up and down.

A fly interrupted whatever I was doing.

"Ew, it's—fucking flew past the camera!" she shrieked.

I slumped down right next to her bedside. "It's gay! It's gay!"

Jack tried to quiet me, "Okay, stop screaming it's fucking—"

I cut her off and then whispered, "It's gonna have sex later and make more baby flies."

Maybe I provided entertainment while blacked out; she always made me feel my opinion and voice mattered. The Hobbit Hole was more than our dwelling; it acted as our little goblin club-house—a piece of our personalities—profoundly broken yet cozy, vibrant, and fun.

(At this precise moment, I hear my boyfriend Brandon breaking the fourth wall to enter the narration and say: "It was the filthiest place I ever stepped into!")

Jack and I would invite coworkers for cocktails and participate in weekend drinking escapades. The Hobbit Hole provided a space of deep reflection. I officially lived free from the church's influence. I could get drunk and come home at whatever time I wanted—free of judgment. The Hobbit Hole was everything short of luxury but proposed cheap rent catering to a pair of broke post-grad-early-twenty-somethings working as gymnastics instructors to make ends meet. We were the perfect roommates, a blend of crazy and fun. We'd make sexual innuendos and swipe Tinder together, gossiping about the boys we wanted to roll in the sheets with. Sometimes, I'd bring men home who'd toss me around my mattress.

Other times, it would be Jack's bed frame banging against the wall and a thunderous chorus of moans, and of course, my drunken Snapchat interpretations: "uh" and "oh" and "ooh."

The Little Big Dogs

S everal months before I broke my ankle, I had no idea what the competition field would look like. In the Fall of 2015, Summit Gymnastics hosted the Washington State Trampoline and Tumbling clinic, where clinicians across the U.S. assembled to coach for the weekend. In attendance were a couple of fourteen-year-old boys who did not fit the profile of your typical gymnast. I imagined they were high school tennis players. Jason had the personality of a Broadway musical star. His teammate Noah brought the energy to fuel the musical theatrics; they both loved singing and dancing and had a Jersey Boys presentation about them. I found it adorable watching them try out gymnastics. But I couldn't wait to show them how talented some actual gymnasts were.

"Alright, everyone," The clinician said. "You're going to run into a round-off, two back handsprings followed by three whips. Got it? Jason, you, alternatively will train transitions!" The clinician looked at his coach and asked, "is he working flick double lay or whip double lay?"

"Both," he said curtly.

Double lay is gym lingo for a double backflip in the straight-body position. The clinician, a coach from Texas, had joked around all afternoon with the athletes to build rapport.

But this time, he wasn't joking.

Jason ran into a perfect round-off back handspring double lay-out on the rod floor, rebounding from the rod floor to his back on a thick sixteen-inch mat to soften the blow. Suddenly, it felt like all the spotlights had turned to shine on me—I had become the athlete everyone in the room viewed as adorable for trying out gymnastics. On the far side of the gym, on a EuroTramp, Noah jumped, and he jumped until he could almost touch the ceiling. His skills were equally impressive. I watched him perform a double front flip in a semi-piked position, with a one-and-a-half twist at the end.

"That's not a pike." His coach said casually.

"I know..."

"Then pike, please."

Jason and Noah were members of the Junior National Team, coached by Neil Hahns, an intense-looking man with an abstract demeanor. Did he hate me? Maybe I felt petrified of his presence because of how brazenly talented his athletes were. Perhaps how he carried himself made me uneasy. The Junior National Team is a bit of a misnomer—"Junior" only means they're not allowed to compete on the senior national team because they're not old enough. You still had to be an elite-level gymnast to be considered a junior. These boys could represent Team USA at the World Championships and even score higher than a few competitors from different countries. To this day, I have only seen a few gymnasts in person compete better than those two could. This clinic presented me with a divine lesson in humility. I would compete for mobility scores to move from level 7 to 10 throughout several meets, a feat Jason and Noah accomplished as middle schoolers. They began their journey to the elite level before I learned how to chuck a layout full-twist into a foam pit.

I competed for the first time in the early spring of 2016 after the doctor cleared me to return to practice. As a sixth grader during the early spring months of 2006, I would have been thrilled at the opportunity to compete in a gymnastics competition as a level 7. Competing ten years later as a twenty-two-year-old level 7 felt odd. Competing in the same flight as a fourteen-year-old kid who tumbled as well as any Olympic gymnast I'd ever seen on YouTube was downright humiliating but oh-so captivating at the same time. This situation wasn't what I imagined when I wrote my sixth-grade yearbook quote. I wanted to be an Olympic gymnast, not compete in the shadow of some Olympic-level kid. Still, I tried to be grateful for the opportunity to accomplish what I had set out to do ten years earlier.

I stood at the beginning of the rod floor, waiting for two others to take their practice pass before I could go. Whitaker walked over. "Alright kid. This will be an easy competition for you—four tumbling passes. A walk in the park."

He was right. My passes were a fucking cakewalk compared to Jason's. I competed round-off, whip, five back handsprings, and dismounted with a simple backflip. Jason's opening pass was five whips, one back handspring to a double-twisting double backflip (two flips, two twists in one skill). I can only accurately explain the vibe of the competition like this: It looked like the scene from a cringy 1994 Disney channel film called Blank Check, where the main character, Preston, is watching his bully, Butch, ride all the cool rides; the roller coaster and the hanging swings spinning high in the sky.

Meanwhile, the scene swiftly juxtaposes Preston riding the toddler rides with tacky music in the background. You could copy and paste the scene. I was Preston at a gymnastics meet.

I competed in levels 7 and 8 at the meet—four tumbling passes back-to-back. Level 8 was more complex but still relatively simple. My first tumbling pass was a round-off whip, five back handsprings to a layout. The next tumbling pass was two whips and four back springs to a layout-full twist. A layout full-twist, the one skill I'd been zealous to accomplish ever since I saw Jennette compete in high school. I viewed the skill as a symbol of hope. If I could fight for five years to figure out how to learn one, I could do anything I set my mind to. By now, it was a compulsory skill for me. In the gym, I could perform at a high level of difficulty, but nowhere near the level Jason or Noah trained—they were on another playing field.

Thankfully, I hit the mobility score I needed to compete at level 9 for my next competition. I was catching up. I coached the rest of the afternoon after winning the competition in my age category (and there wasn't a fight, considering I competed against myself). I watched throughout the evening in amazement as several kids stood off the side crying for one reason or another—a mistake, or maybe they interrupted a routine, or perhaps they were nervous. These kids had the entire world at their fingertips with supportive parents, yet they still found reasons to cry. I wanted to roll my eyes. I reflected on the contrast between these kids raised in wealthy families and the kids like me who weren't as lucky.

Throughout my time at Rogers High School, Mom and Dad never came to watch my track or cross country meets. I only asked them on a handful of occasions to come out and support me. But their excuses were always the same. They were too tired or had no gas money, or Dad couldn't afford to miss a televised football game. During the spring of my senior year in 2012, Gonzaga Prep High School hosted one of my final track meets. We only lived three blocks from Gonzaga Prep, so if an opportunity for them to come to watch presented itself, now was the time.

I asked if they were interested in coming out to watch. I don't remember how they responded. Did they seem excited? Did they seem apprehensive and unsure? I imagine I might have said something like, "Well, If you guys do decide to come out and watch, the track meet starts at four p.m., but you'll want to arrive early!"

The day of the meet came on a cloudy, relatively chilly afternoon; nothing too crazy. Lots of families stood in the cement bleachers, cheering on their athletes. I competed in several races all afternoon. I ran the 800 and the mile, and I'm sure I got lumped into the 4x400 at some point. Mom and Dad both arrived at the meet wearing a blanket, Dad sipping on a bottle of Bud Light he hid. I felt glad they came out to support me. I told my parents I'd be racing the mile later toward the end of the meet.

"Good luck, hun! You've got this!" Mom said as I walked away toward the field.

During my warm-up for the race, I jogged past where my parents sat to see them before I competed, but they walked back home. They didn't watch me run the mile. They watched me compete in one race and then left. When I asked why they left, Mom looked up and said, "You know how your dad is. He just COUDLN'T miss HIS football."

I think about that day all the time.

I got a headache listening to these kids, who got every opportunity they wanted in life handed to them, find ways to act utterly ungrateful. This sport was an opportunity I wish I had growing up. Not only were they ungrateful at the meets, but they also took a laissez-faire approach to practice. They didn't care to put in the work to compete well at the meets. They only wanted to bounce on trampolines and waste time with friends. I often felt like I was herding chickens instead of coaching. But their world ended once the meets rolled around and competition results were less than favorable. It felt like a throat punch—a mockery. Some people didn't have the resources or opportunities to do gymnastics, yet these kids all had this sport presented to them on a silver platter. I wanted to teach them to be grateful for these moments because some people had to fight like hell to get what they wanted.

Despite my resentment toward kids with big emotions, I acted as immature and emotionally volatile, if not more, than they were. A month later, Summit hosted the state championships, my final competition of the year. I clothed myself in a contradictory attitude concerning my gymnastics—mostly apathy and ingratitude. I had always been a problematic athlete, but I took the holier-than-thou approach when working with snotty kids. Whitaker stood to the side of the floor and gave a correction before I went for my practice pass. "Alright. You're up. Remember to reach back and pull your feet in front of you."

I took a shoddy turn, and while walking back with Whitaker, I complained, "I can't tumble on this floor. It's solid as a rock!"

One of the judges at the competition overheard the conversation. "Sounds a lot like user error to me," she joked.

"It's the same floor we have back at the gym," Whitaker added.

"Not even close!"

The rod floor felt soft and bouncy for one half, but the second half felt like marble and made loud sounds as we tumbled. Tumblers sounded like pile drivers firing rapidly. I wanted to engage in a temper tantrum. Again, I found myself competing in the same flight as Jason and another power tumbler, an eight-year-old level 8 named Zed. Zed was also a solid level 9 on Trampoline and double mini—another prodigy of Neil. Zed liked to complain about anything and everything. He was a funny kid, but since he had talent, I enjoyed his antics.

Zed dramatically sprawled on his back. "I can't do this today."

"Zed! Get on the floor and put your passes together!" Neil barked.

"I have a tummy ache."

"You'll be fine, Zed."

Zed was a fast-twitched tumbler, another Jason and Noah in the making. At eight years old, he threw double backs on the rod floor, with Neil's spot—but a double back—nonetheless. Did it feel weird to witness a little kid outcompete me? It felt like another lesson in humility. Neil radiated a no-nonsense approach to coaching. There was nothing wrong with Zed; he had a knack for big theatrics on the competition floor and, as I would soon find out, during practice.

Jason stepped onto the rod floor. I noticed he always straightened his arms and bent his hands like a sloth before he cascaded into his tumbling pass, a technique I dubbed "Jason Hands." I implemented it into my training because, as silly as it seemed, it worked. Whenever Jason took to the floor, whether warming up a pass or competing, everybody in the gym watched, mesmerized by his athletic prowess. He dashed across the floor; "Jason Hands" queued up and hurdled into a round-off with five whips, dismounting a double layout. Whenever I stepped on the rod floor that morning, I felt clunky and unable to navigate my body. I balked at one of my practice passes. I stopped after one whip because I felt crooked and off balance. Feeling off-center wasn't the norm. I could easily connect five whips to a double back tuck at home. Why couldn't I do it here? After three failed practice passes, I had no choice but to compete, unprepared.

Whitaker patted me on the back. "Listen, kid, you've got this. I know you do. You're way better than this. When you step onto the floor, exhale the bullshit, and do what you know you're capable of doing. It's only four whips to a double back tuck!"

I wasn't upset or scared or even nervous. I felt frustrated with my lack of ability to perform what I had trained a thousand times already. I could move on to level 10 next season if I obtained a mobility score at this level. If not, I'd have to begin again as a level 9 the following season. Competing below level 10 felt pointless and silly. I stepped onto the floor and waited for the judge to salute me. Waiting for the judge's salut felt like an eternity every time. The judge saluted me, and I saluted back. I paused momentarily, took a deep breath, straightened my arms, and started running. I focused on the tape mark I stuck to the floor so I'd know where to begin my round-off.

I needed the tape to know where to start my tumbling pass so I'd land my dismount on the yellow and red landing zone. The round-off is the most pivotal skill in the whole pass. It's the easiest, but if I messed it up, I'd likely interrupt the pass mid-routine. My

hands hit the floor with remarkable speed, more than I felt comfortable with. But it propelled me into my whip in a way I hadn't
experienced before. I felt my upper body flying backward, my arms
helped me rotate around, and I pulled my feet around in front of
me before immediately starting my second, third, and fourth whip
on the floor. The complex part of the routine finished, and before
I knew it, I dismounted into a low-to-the-ground double backflip.
Several loud gasps from the spectator section echoed across the
gym as I hit my feet and fell to my back.

Thankfully, I didn't get injured. But I began believing that becoming an elite gymnast wouldn't be possible. I hit a brick wall. I
could tumble decently but far from Jason or Noah. Even Zed could
compete at the same level as me, albeit in different age groups. At
the end of the competition, the meet director awarded me what
felt like a counterfeit first-place finish. Once I got home, I took a
couple of shots of vodka and got ready for a night out on Capitol
Hill.

Carousel of Coaches

The Regional and National championships sailed off the Horizon, and I had yet to qualify to compete at level 10. I reevaluated my goals to focus on obtaining a mobility score to compete from level 10 to elite the following season. I stood firm and let Whitaker know I would only attend Regionals or Nationals if the gym were footing the bill for me to participate as a coach. The next competitive season seemed far enough away; I thought I had time to coast my training for a couple of months to pass time doing what I wanted to do—namely, getting shit-faced at R Place. Whitaker's coaching was effective—he could quickly bring me up to speed in no time. One afternoon, he stood chatting with a beautiful Argentinian woman in the gym lobby.

"This is Sole!" Whitaker announced.

I admired her smile, "Nice to meet you."

"She's gonna be my replacement after I move!"

My eyes grew wide. "Wait you're moving?"

He landed a new job in Connecticut, closer to his family.

Soledad Decca worked as a graphic designer from Indianapolis. She had recently moved to Seattle to coach gymnastics at another local club. When that gym lost its head coach, they handed Sole the program, but she didn't feel ready to take on the position yet. She wanted more time to mentor before taking on the head coach role. In a quick turn of events, she interviewed to coach at King County Gymnastics, quickly becoming an integral part of our program. Sole brought a wealth of knowledge and an ability to click with everybody immediately. She shined bright, with a bubbly personality, and added a lot of warmth into the gym environment, which could sometimes feel cold and distant. Whitaker was a phenomenal coach, but now that he was leaving, he prematurely began phasing out of his role.

"Where is Whitaker?" Sole asked during practice, frustrated.

My coworker Amir looked at Sole, "He's been gone for like three days in a row."

Whitaker's absences were happening more frequently. Since I coached recreational trampoline classes, I had no leeway to help alleviate the slack. Sole and Amir would scramble to keep the practice running efficiently. I wanted to help them with the team, but I couldn't fit it in with my current position as a glorified babysitter. I hated coaching recreational classes and often complained about them; I preferred coaching the team kids. A few weeks later, in a bid for prestige, I interviewed for a position as the manager of the preschool program. I should have brought a robust presence and interviewed better. But I didn't. My boss, Jillian, and another department lead, Ben, could see right through me. I'll never forget what Jillian said, "Kenny, I would love to help support your growth, but I need you to learn how to advocate for yourself."

I left the interview feeling rejected and negatively painted Jillain and Ben. I only made feeble attempts to grow in the area they suggested. Mostly, I gave subtle jabs to the club's culture and incessantly looked for how they were messing up. The truth is Jillian and Ben were right. I didn't know how to advocate for myself. I didn't know how to be a leader. I also enjoyed being on Capitol Hill all night into the early morning. Jillian would have terminated me for not arriving to work on time had I landed the position as the preschool program director.

I stomped up the wooden stairs into the coach's office. "How am I supposed to grow as a coach if they won't give me a chance?" I asked no one in particular.

"I believe in you, Kenny," Sole said. "I see you as technical and patient with your classes."

Sole always lifted everyone's spirits from the get-go. She believed in me even when I sometimes didn't believe in myself.

I stared at the wall. "Am I not knowledgeable enough to coach at this level?"

She closed her notebook. "Don't say that. I've seen how you coach and I know you can do it."

Sole's encouraging words made me enjoy her presence in the gym. She could coach trampoline effectively but didn't partake in the "us versus them" culture that permeated the club. It often felt like the club had two groups: recreational lay staff and the managers. Whitaker had his desk and computer downstairs in the manager's office.

One day, Whitaker entered the recreational coach's office and declared one of the communal computers as Sole's, "She needs it more since she'll be the head trampoline coach moving forward!"

It felt like Whitaker tried stringing Sole along while simultaneously declaring she wasn't enough to be part of the downstairs management crew.

"I wouldn't want to be part of the managers office anyway. We're like a family here," Sole announced after Whitaker left.

I awoke on Monday afternoon, hungover from another weekend escapade around Capitol Hill. I walked to the kitchen, filled a glass of water, and began scrolling through the notifications on my phone. I received an email from Whitaker:

Good morning, team! I have decided to resign from King County Gymnastics effective immediately. I am sorry for this sudden change. I wish you all the best in the future. For all future communication, please see Jillian.

Sole, Amir, and I met in the coach's office several hours later, not saying a word at first, only making eye contact as we shuffled our belongings into our cubbies upstairs. The air felt heavy with anticipation.

Sole broke the ice, "Why did Whitaker resign from his position as the head coach of the T&T program? Does anyone else know?"

Amir sat on the knopparp Ikea couch, "I don't know, but the team parents are going to be mad once they find out!"

Jillian hiked the stairs to the coach's office and poked her head through the door. "Could I have a word with you three in the conference room?" We followed her down the stairs, through the gym, to a separate staircase in the lobby leading to the gym's HR office, the preschool, and an empty multipurpose office. "I assume you guys already know about the situation. I want you all to know I am here to support you and the program," she said empathically.

I wanted to know how this would impact my training, "So, what happens next?"

"Well, right now we are scouring the country to bring another qualified coach to jump into his role. We are searching high and low, but it could be a while before we interview the right candidate."

"Why did he leave?" Sole asked.

"Unfortunately, I can't go into the details of his departure. Ultimately he made the best decision for himself," Jillian continued, "I would like you three to conduct practice and regular classes as if Whitaker never left while I draft a letter and prepare for the parent meeting on Friday. The kids and parents don't know anything about the situation yet, so I'll need you three to keep this under wraps."

The next afternoon, before our shifts began, Jillian pulled Amir and me into another meeting with Sole. "I wanted to touch base with everyone to go over the plan—at least temporarily until we can find another coach." She looked us both in the eyes, "Moving forward, Sole will be the program lead! I am confident in her managerial ability; I believe she is the right fit to take charge of the program."

I nodded along, feeling defeated.

"Amir," Jillian continued, "I'd like for you to continue co-coaching the team with Sole. I am going to take you off the remainder of your recreational classes and hand them over to Kenny so we can stay afloat while we look for a head coach." She looked at me. "Kenny, I would love for you continue training with the team, but right now, we need all hands on deck for a while. You'll need to coach the extra recreational classes during your training time."

I wasn't okay with this plan at all. I had been coaching at King County Gymnastics for several years. Jillian knew I wanted to coach team classes. This situation created the perfect opportunity for me to step into the role. Instead, she gave me more recreational T&T classes to teach. I sunk into my chair, "Would there still be another way for me to at least train?"

"Of course, you could still attend the coaches' gym on Wednesday nights."

Sole looked at me, "I'd be willing to stay an hour after practice to make sure you could still have time to practice."

Sole jumped into the chaos, motivated and ready to ensure everyone felt successful moving forward. But I had reservations about her. Did she have the qualifications to coach me? Could I trust her to coach me?

"What about the team kids and their families?" Amir asked, "what are we going to tell them?"

Jillian sighed, "There's no easy answer, but the next thing on our agenda will be a parent meeting on Friday after practice. Tell the kids Whitaker is on vacation for the week if they ask about his whereabouts. I don't want rumors circulating."

On Friday, the three of us convened upstairs in the preschool for one of several parent meetings. The first parent directed their attention to Jillian, "What actions are you taking to find a qualified coach to replace Whitaker?"

"We are doing everything in our power to recruit. We have several candidates whom we are actively scheduling interviews with."

"What about the meantime? How are you going to progress our kids without proper coaching?"

"Together," Jillian said, making eye contact with the three of us, "Sole, Amir, and Kenny will all be stepping up in big ways to ensure your athletes continue to thrive in this sport."

"Are they even qualified to coach at this level?" Another parent scoffed.

The first parent quickly interjected again, "How are a bunch of early twenty-something kids realistically going to make sure my daughter continues receiving adequate training at her level?"

Jillian maintained a calm and professional demeanor, never wavering once in her conviction. She always had an answer for everything and went to bat for us." I am confident in their ability to coach high quality gymnastics," Jillian said, looking at Sole.

"I may be young," Sole said, "but I competed as an elite-level trampolinist, raised in the sport. I have the tools at my disposal to move forward with your gymnast's progress."

It became immediately apparent which parents trusted us and which ones had little to no faith in us.

"Well, I'm not confident in this situation at all. We will be unenrolling our daughter from your program effective immediately," the first parents said, storming out the door. We could hear their ferocious stomps from the staircase.

Jillian fixed her gaze on the rest of the parents sitting before us. "We will offer tuition refunds for this month to anyone else who wishes to do the same."

In the end, a few families decided to leave the club. Sole and Amir jumped in as the architects prepared to restore the team to its former glory. They were, indeed, the right coaches to put on the team. They took charge of the program in monumental ways, showing the team parents precisely who they were and what they were capable of. I felt like my coaching paled in comparison.

Amir insisted on giving the kids drills to perfect their skills; he was also an effective spotter, spotting the gymnasts ready to toss double-flipping Salto's on the trampoline. Sole was an organized leader and equally brilliant with her technical training at the higher levels. With everything happening, I saw myself as a relatively dispensable part of the Trampoline and Tumbling program. I wanted to rank higher on the ladder than a fill-in for the recreational classes. Despite how I felt about the situation, we were a well-oiled machine, keeping the program streaming ahead. But I second-guessed myself a lot. Was I a fraud? What was the point of coaching if my role forever remained the same? I looked at the situation as a sufficient reason to get drunk.

I walked into work hungover, holding the Mocha I ordered from Woodland Coffee. Sole was packing her belongings upstairs, preparing to join the downstairs management team.

"This is the second time this has happened to me," she somberly said as I shoved my backpack into an empty cubby.

I looked over at her. "What is?"

"A head coach leaving and the entire program getting dumped into my lap. I wanted the opportunity to mentor under elite-level coaches. I looked forward to Whitaker's mentorship."

I rolled closer to her while sitting in the computer chair. "Maybe everything happens for a reason. Maybe this is like a sign you're supposed to be in this position?"

"You think?"

"It's tough to say. But I often feel like I keep going through shitty situations like this. I don't enjoy coaching recreational gymnastics—I hate it. it's not fun, and it's not rewarding," I paused to reflect, "But maybe there's a grand purpose for all of this!"

I was jealous of Sole and Amir. I felt like they had all these incredible opportunities handed to them, and I got breadcrumbs. Neither Sole nor Amir realized I harbored this resentment. Not towards them, but the situation. I never said anything because I wanted to feel happy about their success. We were all in the trenches together, growing as budding humans. I continued to dwell on my plight. Why couldn't Whitaker have stayed a little bit longer? We were doing so well together. I started making so much progress in the sport under him. Did Sole have what it took to take me to the next level? I wasn't so sure. But she continued to stand in my corner through the whole ordeal. She was so supportive, even after taking the reins of the entire program. She never made me feel like her subordinate. She made the program feel like a tight-knit family. She tried to make light of a shitty situation. But my melancholy was prevalent at times.

I sat on the knopparp Ikea couch. "This is the second time something like this has also happened to me."

"Really?"

"I was training college gymnastics for a bit, and things were awesome, but then my church presented an ultimatum, and they basically forced me to quit. I quit gymnastics until I found the courage to leave the church. I only saw my way back into the sport through Whitaker. Now he's gone."

What was I supposed to learn from this? During this transition, I never thought to self-reflect. Was I prepared to take on the challenges of becoming a program leader? I thought I was, but it never occurred to me that I still had many more areas of growth and maturity to discover. My arrogance blinded me.

Into the Darkness

After a wild summer in a perpetual blackout, I returned to training gymnastics a couple of nights per week under Sole's direction. Sole transitioned from being my friend and colleague to my boss and coach overnight. Negative feelings clouded my judgment and prevented me from fully trusting her. Mainly, I felt disappointed I didn't receive the same opportunities. I felt like King County Gymnastics repeatedly passed me over, pushing me into the same role I had from the beginning: recreational-instructor-and-sometimes-birthday-party-host.

Sole pulled me in for a meeting in the manager's office twenty minutes before I started coaching. "I'm sensing a disconnect between us. I'm not sure what going on. Talk to me."

I sat in silence for some time. I looked over at the ticking analog clock with Roman numerals. "I don't feel like I'm being taking seriously at this gym."

Sole clasped her hands together and sat up straighter. "I can see that."

I could only focus on the ticking as I looked down at the table before making eye contact with Sole. "Yeah. It's frustrating. Sometimes I don't want to coach here anymore."

"If it makes you feel any better, I think you're a stellar coach. You're detail oriented and so patient with the little ones. I can talk to Jillian to see about putting you on one of the team classes."

I perked up, "you will?"

I wanted to be grateful for Sole's effort but couldn't. As soon as I began coaching the team, I felt too good for them; I wanted more. The group they assigned me to coach felt like a glorified recreational class but longer. Much longer. Many kids had zero work ethic, took few turns during practice, and played around when they were supposed to listen to instructions. Right out of the gate, I got super annoyed with this group. My new predicament only further reinforced my disdain. The new team group was my lesson in positive coaching. Coaches like me are supposed to champion their team culture, and already, I was messing it up. The year before, I had a lot of hope for my budding career as a coach. Now, I wanted to quit. But I still needed a job to survive, and gymnastics was all I knew, all I felt proficient at. It was as if my passion for the sport faded with each passing day.

My interests became centered around being part of the adventure throughout Capitol Hill. The Hill was a neighborhood of connection and belonging for a community often in crisis. We were struggling to understand the reasons for the Pulse Night Club shooting. The tragedy forced gay bars to tighten their security protocols. The result made members of our community often feel like perpetrators instead of patrons as security checked bags for guns. Still, LGBTQ pride was a shining symbol of the Hill, most prevalent during Pride Month in June. Rainbow flags lined businesses along Broadway Street; activists sometimes broke into community-supported peaceful protests.

The Hill felt like a reprieve from the frustrations of gymnastics and my hectic schedule at the gym, offering a space to grapple with my ever-changing identity. Maybe competing in gymnastics wasn't for me anymore. Still, it was challenging to conceptualize what life could be like apart from the sport. I wanted to spend my free time drunk on Capitol Hill, not thinking about gymnastics. The allure of gay nightlife in Seattle always had me feeling elated. Perhaps my purpose in life was getting drunk. After all, I did catch an Uber home to R Place almost nightly.

The Uber rides and bar tabs kept adding every month. But so did my unpaid competition fees and resentment for King County Gymnastics. The front desk registrar reminded me about my outstanding competition fees every week. But I didn't care anymore. I knew I couldn't afford the bill and deliberately skipped the payments. After all, comp fees didn't get me drunk; alcohol did. Gymnastics didn't alleviate the feelings of doom and dread I experienced; alcohol did. I wanted to be out drinking as early as my schedule permitted, spending money I didn't have, dilating the debt hole, and ready to give birth to financial ruin. I drank tequila shots with a chaser if I became stressed by my finances. If I became anxious about eternal torment, I drank it without.

Inside the third-floor bathroom at R Place, I stood with a small group of pretty girls. One by one, the girl to my left placed a key into a small baggy covered in Halloween Bats and lifted a white powder at the edge of the key for everyone to sniff. I had never done cocaine before, but buzzed and feeling less inhibited, I decided I'd give it a try. The brunette girl with flawless skin and the ability to read the newbie in the room held the key to my left nostril, closed my right with her thumb, and said, "Now sniff!"

Sniffed, I did.

What had I done?

What initial guilt I might have experienced entirely became overshadowed by the fact I suddenly wanted to be anybody and everybody's absolute number one friend. I became the most talkative person in the group. Was this what cocaine did for people? I didn't want to stop. I started with one or two bumps but quickly escalated to asking around, publicly, where to find some of my own. A few weeks later, Jack caught on to my shenanigans; she pulled me aside with a stark warning:

"You cannot do that, Kenny. It's highly illegal, and you could get arrested. Not to mention getting stuff laced with Fentanyl which can kill you! Yuh dumb, dumb!" She said, hitting me in the head lightly.

After cocaine entered the picture, I stopped doing chores around the Hobbit Hole, frequently contributed to messes, and often came home blacked out and high. Our friendship began taking a wound. We fought over my ill-advised words or actions while under the influence; then I'd quietly slip into bed, wake up the next afternoon feeling like shit, left to wonder about my actions the night before. Still, I viewed life as a party and intended to keep it this way. My spending habits and alcohol consumption were out of control. I reasoned I needed the substances to feel free from my inner righteous Christian conscience. Though it had been a few years since I stopped attending church on Sundays, I still felt like I had never left. I felt trapped in a weird in-between I didn't fully understand. No matter how far away from the church

I tried to run, I couldn't ditch the dreaded feeling of going to Hell. The ICOC had intricately trapped me in a set of beliefs, and now I was turning to cocaine and alcohol to cope with the trauma. In doing so, I dug myself further into debt. Going under the influence was the only way to free myself from the prison of my mind. It also consequently allowed me to not worry about my bank account.

I hit my credit card limit in front of a bartender I routinely flirted with while drunk.

"Do you have another card? This one is saying declined."

"What? That's not possible. I have like a $2,000 credit limit," I said, handing him my debit card.

Meanwhile, I checked my bank account. On my phone screen, I saw I had blown through my credit card limit. If I wanted to continue partying, I needed to figure something else out quickly. I only used my debit card for fixed expenses like rent or the cell phone bill. However, I remained addicted to the fast-paced lifestyle of the night. I wanted to sip on cocktails and quietly slip away to snort key bumps with strangers. But now, I couldn't rely on my credit card for a night out. Thankfully, I kept the lessons I learned from Mom and Dad as a kid. In the early 2000s, sometimes money was tight at home. I always knew because our fridge would be empty, the cable would stop working, or Avista utilities would cut off our electricity, leaving us in the dark. After a few days, they'd take me to run errands. We'd park in the lot of a Money Tree near the NorthTown Mall, and they would cheerfully return to the car after fifteen minutes. Later in the day, the power would get restored, the cable turned on, and I could open the door to a fridge full of food. My parent's budgeting strategy had become my own—I'd borrow from Money Tree.

The lights on R Place's dance floor were blinding. Several people lollygagged in line, waiting to order their next drink of the night. As a community, the weekends were what bound us together. We lived in a straight world, but once Thursday night rolled around, we could jump into a tiny gay oasis of drag queens, go-go boys, White Claws, and random shots of tequila from strangers.

"Whadya want Strange?" The bartender asked.

"Can I get an AMF?"

"EW!" He yelled jokingly. "The fuck you want one of those for?"

I smiled innocently. "Uhh I don't know. I want to try one."

Short for Adios Mother Fucker, the bartender handed me the blue drink garnished with a maraschino cherry on top. I gave him cash from the funds I borrowed from Money Tree earlier in the afternoon.

"Here you go, Strange! Now get the fuck out of here!"

The AMF tasted like motor oil, but I wanted to look like somebody who knew how to drink, not a soft gay boy who only ordered gumdrops and lollipops for cocktails. If I were going to drink, I would do it right, not like the namby pamby I used to be when I started coming out. I began to rebrand myself. I stumbled over to the stage and observed everyone dancing. I saw straws flailing out of cups and beverages splashing onto the floor. Toxic by Britney Spears played over the speakers. I wanted to dance the night away with everyone else.

The music stopped, and the DJ announced over the loudspeakers, "Alright! It's time to clear the stage. Grab another cocktail, and don't forget to tip your bartenders because they'll be taking care of you all night long."

One of R Places' resident drag queens sashayed onto the stage wearing a white frilled leotard with thigh-high heeled boots and a long brown wig. She twirled, danced, and jumped into splits while lip-synching; the bar went wild watching her performance.

After her number ended, she grabbed the microphone from the DJ and then screamed, "How the fuck are y'all doing tonight? It's Thirsty Thursday here at R Place, and we're going to get ready for the amateur strip contest! I need some volunteers!"

I can only reconstruct the events from that night through a video I watched from a guy who recognized me later in the week- end. While blacked out, I got volunteered by someone to enter the amateur strip contest who pushed me onto the stage.

I imagine I whispered, "fuck it, I'm drunk."

The drag queen looked up at the DJ's booth, "DJ, start the music!"

Ariana Grande's *Into You* blasted through the speakers; I wig- gled my hips and tried to look sexy and seductive. But the reality looked like a five-year-old learning to Hula Hoop. While dancing, I awkwardly pulled my shirt off, bounced around in circles, and then changed the rhythm. I danced Gangnam-style before pulling out some floppy fish jumps. Ultimately, I decided to do a backflip on the stage, slamming my feet into the floor and falling over to my back. Uninjured but hopelessly intoxicated, I jumped back to my feet, and the small crowd went wild. The music cut right after I fell; I didn't win the amateur strip contest per se, but I walked away with a seventy-five-dollar cash prize, enough to cover my tab for the evening.

Despite Jack's warnings, I graduated from key bumps and lines from strangers in a bathroom to purchasing little baggies. Life felt euphoric in those moments, and I believed myself invincible. If the drinks made me feel tired, the cocaine brought me to an alert mind. I could talk to anyone about anything. I stopped acting as an introverted wallflower observing the environment. I was the environment.

Until I awoke the next afternoon to an internalized crushing sensation in my chest that I had never experienced before. Was this because I maxed out my credit card? Was it because I did drugs? Could this also be what a hangover felt like? Was it God calling me to repentance? The heaviness was deafening. I never realized I could feel this way. Was this what depression felt like? Why do I feel this way? The feelings of sadness and doom intermixed and made me rethink all my choices in life.

I took an Uber to church. Again.

Joshua recognized me the moment I walked through the doors. He looked surprised yet excited to see me in the sanctuary. "Kenny! What is up, man? So glad to see you here!"

I leaned against the pew. "I can't keep taking this path I'm on, anymore. I am drinking myself to death."

Joshua knew me better than most people in the church. He knew my highs and lows but never made me feel less than. He seemed genuine.

"Why don't you come back to a Bible Talk with us tomorrow? I'll even drive you over!"

"Count me in."

"You'd be making the right choice, Kenny," Joshua sat in the pew beside me, "The church has changed since you left."

"Has it?"

"Come sit down, man!" He moved a bible away to make room for me. "Yeah, we've grown a lot as a congregation. We've repented of the things hurting you in the past."

"Oh, okay," I look over at him, unbelieving. "I don't want to go to Hell. That's the path I'm on now, and I think God is warning me."

I didn't believe him about the church changing. I knew I would have to repent of all my sins. All the biblical rules are what made me hate the church. But at this point, I only wanted the sadness to flee me. I arrived at the Bible Talk, still recovering from the fear and anxiety-ridden hangover from the weekend. I confessed to doing cocaine, which made me feel right again with God. Being around disciples always lifted the weight of going to Hell; this felt like confirmation from God. Did he feel pleased with my decision to return? The ICOC had trapped me on a carousel of condemnation and redemption. God condemned me each time I stepped into a gay bar and then redeemed me each time I returned to the church. The hangover felt like God's latest attempt to save me again.

I felt confident in my decision. "I want to get restored. I'm ready to leave my old life behind."

"Eh! That's great, Kenny!" Joshua said.

After hearing the news, several people came to congratulate me. I felt like I was restarting. I could feel the love-bombing tactics creeping over. Another former roommate at the Wingate came over to me, "I'm encouraged by you, Kenny. Your story is deepening my faith. Your testimony is going to be a powerful influence in the kingdom!"

One coke-induced panic attack, and suddenly, I wanted to live as a disciple again. Was that all it took? I hesitated to leave homosexuality again, but I was dreadfully committed to diving back into the throes of discipleship.

Off the Deep End

My faith and the intercepting battle with homosexuality were causing me to go manic. I couldn't get over the dilemma. Too often, the crash from my drinking and cocaine use compounded feelings of desperation, bringing me back to church. I'd read through the whole Bible. I believed in the ICOC's theology. I'd done this dance before but hated every minute of it. So why did I want to return to this church so bad? To an impractical lifestyle? I didn't want to be a disciple again. But the idea of going to Hell fucking frightened me.

When I initially left the church, I told myself my splurge in the LGBTQ community would come to an end at some point. I believed I would become a faithful church member again—wiser than before. I just didn't think the end would come so quickly. Would I be strong enough to stave off the pieces of me that didn't align with the ICOC's interpretation of the Bible? Despite wanting to go out and get drunk on the weekends, I remained sober and continued attending church on Sundays.

During my initial restoration study, I discussed how perverted and deeply flawed I had become in the world.

I looked over at Joshua. "I can feel God calling me to repentance! I want my life back!" I started crying. Did I feel this way about my circumstances, or was I trying to be dramatic? Maybe this was my desperate attempt to convince myself that discipleship was what I needed to live happily ever after.

Joshua opened his Bible and fumbled through its worn pages to quote a scripture from Psalms. He said he could feel God calling me to repentance, too. He told me he believed God had been calling me away from my rebellion for some time. But I had already failed God once. Who's to say I wouldn't do it again? Worse, what if God's intent all along was to condemn me to Hell?

Mitch took immediate control of the subsequent restoration study. I didn't enjoy Mitch's influence in my life. He came across as arrogant. Mitch opened the study with a cookie-cutter prayer, thanking God for our time together and how grateful he felt to be here studying the Bible with me. His inflection made me want to throat-punch him. Instead, I made it a point to show apathy and disregard for his opinions about my spirituality.

"How are you feeling today, Kenny?" Mitch asked.

I shrugged my shoulders. "The same. I feel cruddy. I don't know. Living as a disciple doesn't feel natural."

"Life as a disciple isn't natural. It goes against the grain of societal standards. Society wants you to go out, drink, party and even sleep around. They celebrate it and wear it like a badge. But we—and that includes you, Kenny—are called higher than that."

I gave a knowing glance. "I know what I need to do to get right with God. I lived faithfully as a disciple before, remember? Tell me something I don't already know."

He looked at me arrogantly. "And... where's your faith in all of this?"

I tried to mimic his demeaning tone. "Where do you think my faith is? Look, life as a disciple is easier for people like you who don't struggle with un-fucking-wanted same-sex attraction."

Mitch put his elbows on the table, "I don't know if I agree with that, Kenny. We all have our personal struggles to deal with. You're not the only person to struggle with sexual temptation."

I repositioned myself in my chair. "It runs deeper than sexual temptation. Straight men, like yourself, can get married to their girlfriends and are free to have all the sex they want after the fact."

Mitch flipped through his Bible. "Do you think heterosexual brothers won't think about wanting sexual relations with women who aren't their wives?"

"That's not relevant. They can still fuck their wives and not be in sin—"

His finger pointed irreverently in my direction. "Language!"

"All I'm saying is you have a church-approved sexual outlet. I do not. What am I supposed to do with these overbearing temptations?"

He maintained eye contact with me. "You pray about them! Like I've said before, God could change your heart. Have you been praying about this?"

"What do you think?"

Joshua, likely sensing the tension, chimed in from across the table. "We could all pray together if you'd like."

My unwanted sexual urges felt like a punishment from God. But for what? What had I done to deserve this? Why couldn't I have been born heterosexual like most men? The road to Heaven felt impossible. After the study ended, Mitch and I spent another hour together, reading and dissecting the scriptures regarding homosexuality and its harm to disciples. His final comment of the evening caught me off guard.

"You could get AIDS. Is this what you want? To die from AIDS as a punishment from God?"

From the day I first met him, Mitch rubbed me the wrong way. Now, I shuddered at his comments. He had no regard for the LGBTQ community. I stood to address him, "I can't fully commit to the teachings of this God-forsaken church."

He leaned back. "Why is that, can I ask?"

"Because I'm not happy. My faith is the entire framework of my existence here on earth, and it fucking sucks!"

Mitch stuffed his Bible into his backpack. "I feel better living my life for Christ."

"Well I don't! I would prefer to set myself on fire than live the rest of my life this way. You're not being asked to be celibate for the rest of your life!"

"Quit putting God in a box." Mitch said sharply. "He can find you a girlfriend and you could get married, too!"

I rolled my eyes.

"You're right, Kenny. Maybe I don't understand what it's like. You know, I'm not even sure it's a valid struggle at this point. You know the commands, but you willingly continue your little pity parties. That, my friend, is your own fault."

Mitch was the type of guy who proclaimed love for people, but I could see right through him. He had no love for me or my community. I replayed his AIDS comment. Was this what God wanted for me?

Fuck this.

Capitol Hill was my refuge, not the ICOC.

It was a warm afternoon as I walked through Cal Anderson Park. I saw people throwing frisbees, chasing their dogs off-leash, and lying in the grass in small groups. Would leaving the LGBTQ community be worth all this pain I was bound to suffer again? I couldn't grapple with what my future as a disciple would look like. I remembered my time in the ICOC. I remembered the struggle and how often I loathed who I was as a person. Denying my sexual orientation felt dishonest. Perhaps—for a moment, I could do both. Maybe I could lead a double life? Would God have grace on me because he could see my attempts at biblical discipleship? He knew what I was fighting against, didn't He? My life felt like a daily litmus test for my readiness for the kingdom of God. My desire to be myself heavily outweighed my desire to be a disciple. I wanted to be in a relationship with another man, and no amount of praying to God, seeking God, or denying myself was changing that.

I exited Cal Anderson Park and walked past Molly Moons, an ice cream parlor on the corner of 10th Ave and E Pine Street. I wanted an ice cream cone. R Place also called my name. The bar stood only three blocks down E Pine St. While munching a chocolate ice cream cone, I decided the ICOC didn't get to define me, and it didn't get to dictate my actions. Mitch didn't get to have any power over my life. But the gravitational pull—the indoctrination from the church was powerful enough to bring me back, time and time again. It would only be a matter of time before I would return to the church again for forgiveness. I wanted to break free from captivity. I wanted to stop suffering from this illusion the

ICOC presented of freedom. I wasn't free. Why couldn't I escape the clutches of the church? I'd clench my fists thinking about the psychological torment the ICOC put me through. I wanted nothing to do with God or Christianity.

I promptly returned to getting shitfaced at R Place. I knew I'd feel right at home at the bar, especially after undergoing a little church-related turmoil. I must have been addicted to the toxic cycle. At least with bars, drinking alcohol provided me with a social lubricant and a way to cope with my crippling religious trauma.

As soon as I walked through the side door of the club, the bartender greeted me. "Eh, Strange! What are you drinking?"

"Umm I'll take a Vodka cran and a shot of Absolut!" I said, feeling mature in my beverage orders.

"You got it! That'll be $16."

It always took me less than five minutes to finish the first drink. I never drank to enjoy a cocktail; I drank to get drunk. After guzzling the first cocktail, I sauntered up to the bar.

"You're back! You want another?"

"Yasss!" I said, over-accentuating the lisp.

"Alright. Here you go, Strange!"

After several drinks, I felt plastered enough to snort key bumps with girlfriends in the parking lot across the street from the club. Later, I wandered to the third floor to dance with a random guy I met who sat at the bar alone. He was visiting Seattle from Texas, he said. Our dancing looked about as close to sex as you could get on the dance floor—shirts off, warm hands sliding in and out of trousers, tongues sliding back and forth, never fully knowing whose gum this was, to begin with.

"Would you like a glass of water?" The bartender asked after we returned to the bar for a breather and another drink.

"No, I'll take some vodka," I said, drunk, giggles coming out, leaning against my fuck bud for the night.

"How about some water?"

"How about Vodka!"

"Sorry, Strange. I gotta cut you off for now. Sober up and I'll be glad to serve you again."

The bartenders at R Place always knew when to cut me off. They knew because I turned into a mess. I am also profoundly ingrained with habits: always going to the same bars, sitting in the same seats, and, for the most part, ordering the same drinks and offering the same drunk compliments like "I think you're so sexy!" without missing a beat.

If I became a drunk mess at R Place, my inebriation followed me home to the Hobbit Hole. Spending six, sometimes seven nights a week on Capitol Hill, I frequently came home, beyond blacked out, while Jack watched TV. She reconstructed the story for me the following afternoon. She told me that I came home drunk, opened the front door, and, with an accent, said, "I'm back."

She looked over at me, "You're drunk. Go to bed."

"Listen here, bitch!" I shuffled over to lean into the armchair, "I am not even drunk at all."

"You're so drunk you can't even stand straight."

"Oh my God guess what?"

"Your eyes are looking right through me."

"Wait, guess what." I said, tilting into the armchair.

"What?"

"I had sex... with a girl!"

"What? Shut the fuck up, no you didn't."

"Yes, I did! I came all over the walls at the club!"

"Okay, it's time for some water, and off to bed, you go!"

"I love you, bitch!"

"I love you, too. Now Go to bed!"

I have no memory of this. When I woke up the next afternoon, my plummeting financial situation ransacked my brain. Every trip to R Place added another expense. Each time I went out, I spent money I didn't have, deepening my debt. I stressed out over my bleak financial plight, only to further bring myself to spend more on drinks. After I maxed out my credit card in addition to the Payday loans from Money Tree, I began racking yet another source of debt through an app that allowed me to access my paychecks early. The app would send as much as one hundred dollars daily to my bank account anytime I wanted. It would send me up to five hundred dollars per pay period. The overdue amount would get subtracted from my bank account once I got paid. Mismanaging my finances would eventually be my downfall. I couldn't possibly come back from all these sources of debt. I didn't make enough. My finances, like my life and apartment, were an utter mess.

I continued neglecting chores around the Hobbit Hole and kept a messy bedroom. Sometimes, after a house party, liquor bottles, empty beer cans, and greasy pizza boxes would line our trash can before Jack eventually took them all out herself. The messes never bothered me; I had grown accustomed to them during childhood.

Most mornings, I trekked five blocks across snow-trodden side-walks to Longfellow Elementary. It was a bright sunny morning, and the snow glistened in the distance like white marble in the untouched frozen yards of the houses I passed. As soon as the bell rang at 9:00 a.m. for the morning, the teachers greeted students from each entryway. My fourth-grade reading and writing teacher, Mrs. X, wasn't in a delightful mood this morning, thanks to the class's behavior with the substitute teacher the previous day.

"Never," she snarled, "In my 28 years of teaching, have I ever received such a rotten note about a class from a substitute!"

She ranted while berating various troublemakers. I was sick the previous day and hadn't witnessed the sheer horror she raved about. You would have thought the class had committed some heinous crime. Nope. The issue arose from students who wouldn't stop talking or couldn't stay in their seats. Mrs. X, tired of our class's behavior, mine in particular, walked over with a frown. I didn't assume I could be her target.

She grabbed my desk and pulled it away from me.

Whoosh!

She forcefully scattered all the contents of my desk across the carpet in front of the entire class. The room went into an uproar. I felt publicly crucified by my peers.

"Ew!"

"gross!"

"Yuck!"

"Nasty!"

Their condemnations echoed through the classroom, bouncing off the walls and smacking me. Embarrassment filled me like the ethanol in a liquid thermometer. To this day, I believe she intentionally did this to shame me.

"Now," she said in her most pleasant voice, "clean it up! Nobody's desk should ever be as messy as yours! I can only imagine what your bedroom looks like!"

I would have never admitted it to her, but my bedroom looked messy. We had a mice problem; the mice lived under the floorboards and sometimes scuttled through my room, squeaking every so often. My bedroom sat in the basement because I couldn't stop wetting the bed at night, and by now, I had permanently soaked my mattress in urine. The mattress was an old twin bed, so old coils poked out of the padding—a hand-me-down from my brother and sister. I had to lay a towel down to sleep on something dry and keep it from poking me. I collected trash, dirty clothes, and old dishes for weeks because I felt too lazy to take them upstairs to wash them.

Still, I felt unsure what I did to provoke Mrs. X to humiliate me like this. I wanted to cry. But I knew the adage: boys don't cry. Crying would only aggravate the situation.

Jack sometimes defended me; other times, she called me out. I wasn't a kid anymore; I had no intention of letting adults tell me what to do or how to live my life. I told myself I didn't need Jack to yell at me over how I conducted myself while drunk. One time, Jack hosted friends at the Hobbit Hole. Everyone drank while having a cheerful time until I became intoxicated enough to ruin the vibe. I leaned into one of Jack's friends, making her feel uncomfortable.

Jack looked at me. "You're making Elina feel uncomfortable. Can you give her some space, please?"

I looked at Jack, then looked at her friend and leaned in even closer. "It's okay because I'm gay!"

"No, It's not. You need to stop!" She snapped at me.

"Like I said... I'm gay, It's fine." I babbled again.

"Kenny!"

When she confronted me the next day, I responded, "It's not like I was coherent!"

I had become accustomed to disregarding how others felt during childhood, and now, as an adult, drinking exacerbated the issues running deep. The transaction between me and Mrs. X this day likely wasn't unwarranted. I created distractions and went out of my way to relentlessly target kids by being as annoying as I could—because in my mind—I was funny. It was a particular way of entertaining myself because everything about life felt monotonous and boring. I didn't do well in school due to my inner chaos and lack of academic ambition. I was hyper-fixated about becoming a gymnast, and spending hours in a classroom did not support my aspirations.

Mrs. X had an accountability chart with every student's name written above a clear pocket housing a series of solid-colored cards meant to be shuffled around based on behavioral expectations for the day. Everyone started the day with a green card and a clean slate, and if it didn't get pulled, it meant a student was on their behavior for the day. Suppose Mrs. X said to draw a card; a yellow lurked beneath the green. Yellow meant a warning for the day; it was time to collect yourself. Underneath the yellow card was a red card—an automatic phone call to home or mom's work. The red card was the color I dreaded pulling the most. It was also the card I usually pulled before the end of the day. A red card meant listening to the *swoosh* of Dad's belt as it glided through the belt loops as he bent me over his knee. Mrs. X sometimes told me my parents were lazy and lacked disciplinary action toward me—the reason, she said, I acted the way I did. If they weren't discipling me, what were they doing? If the belt wasn't disciplinary action enough, what was enough?

I was a problematic child at Longfellow, and my teachers did what they could to handle my hyperactivity. As an adult, I began taking inventory of my character. I noticed I hadn't matured from the time I was a kid at Longfellow. The only difference between then and now was how I coped. I was abandoning my passion for gymnastics, which previously carried me through each day. Instead, I was turning to drugs and alcohol for comfort. I was becoming the person I promised never to become. I remembered my conversation with Dad in Walla Walla after we visited with Lynn. I'd broken my promise.

Alcohol drowned my negative feelings. Cocaine gave me the confidence to occupy space. Was I in financial ruin? Was I going to Hell? Yes, but It didn't matter to me so long as I was six shots and three lines deep. Drinking and snorting provided fun vibes all around. Was I feeling happy? I'd get buzzed. Was I stressed or anxious? I'd get drunk. Was I feeling bored or lonely? I'd black out.

In 2001, I had a dream that Mrs. X slapped me across the face, then grabbed me by the shoulder and started shaking me back and forth. I woke not to Mrs. X but to an earthquake shaking the house's walls. I was too tired to register what was happening. A slew of earthquakes ripped through Spokane that year. Even before Mrs. X became my teacher, she represented punishment. My first-grade teacher always sent me to her class when I acted out. I noticed Mrs. X was a strict and exacting woman, even toward the kids in her second-grade class at the time. She demanded her students walk in two lines side by side, claiming one long snake of students was messy and disorganized. She could also quickly correct any misgivings in the lines if students walked on ice.

For years, Mrs. X haunted me in my dreams. As a kid, the nightmares were physical punishment. As an adult, I'd dream of seeing myself in the mirror, suddenly seeing Mrs. X instead of my reflection, looking directly at me, mocking me.

"You broke your promise! You're just like Lynn and you'll never amount to anything!"

The apple never does fall far from the tree. It hadn't now.

I kept training in gymnastics, but barely. My desire to be great in the sport vanished. I became an empty shell continuing in a sport I no longer enjoyed. I wanted to quit, but I wasn't ready to admit that. What was the purpose of having hope in something if it always led to letdowns and heartbreak? To cope with this new sense of loss, I drunkenly indulged myself in a long string of hookups with strangers I met at the club or a bathhouse. Night after night, I gave myself to unprotected sexual encounters, thinking the pleasure might be what life was about. I didn't need gymnastics. I needed to drink and fuck.

Once, While drunk at a bathhouse, a stranger told me he was HIV positive and undetectable. I wasn't sober enough to consent, and we had sex. My intoxication was the only reason we fucked. The truth is one I'm not proud of. I was not above discriminating against HIV-positive individuals. I only had a preconceived notion of what it meant to live with HIV. One time, I went on a date with a guy who disclosed his HIV status. I promptly ghosted him. *Don't have sex with people like him,* I thought. I lived with the knowledge I might now be living with HIV. I didn't know that undetectable meant untransmittable. Was I going to die? Was this the end of my dating and social life in the LGBTQ community? I only understood HIV illuminated by the stigma surrounding it. Instead of making an appointment at a clinic and educating myself further, I continued to drown myself in more alcohol, more cocaine, and more random hookups.

When Christmas rolled around, I took a two-week trip to visit my parents in Spokane. I got drunk every night and acted like everything in my life was perfect. Things weren't okay; I wasn't okay. On the final night before returning home, I sat in the living room with Dad, kicking back a BudLight. Something changed in him that night. He looked over at me and kept telling me over and over how sorry he was for the way he treated me as a kid. How he wished he could take it all back. I wasn't sure how to react.

Then, with tears in his eyes, he looked at me and, cracking his voice, said, "And I am so proud of you, son! So, so proud of you!"

It was one of the first times I'd seen Dad cry. It was the first time I felt seen. Like the essence of who I am as a person mattered to him. It was an emotional end to my trip with Dad. I made a mental note to become a better roommate and prepare to face my uncertainty when I returned to Seattle after New Year's. *New year; new me.*

I returned to Seattle late and rode back to the Hobbit Hole. The next day, Jack knocked at my bedroom door around 2:00 p.m. to wake me up. "We need to talk when you're ready," she said through the door.

I groggily opened my door, walked over, and sat beside her on the couch.

"Hey. So," Jack took a breath before continuing, "While you were gone, I walked into your bedroom to hide my boyfriend's Christmas present. When I opened your door; I'm not exaggerating when I say this—a cloud of fruit flies wafted out, and hit me in the face!"

"Uh... okay." I said, unbothered.

"Kenny!" she barked, "You had a half-eaten rotisserie chicken on your floor! And several water bottles full of piss next to your bed!"

I cocked my head and shrugged my shoulders. "That's not my fault, Jackie! They were in the kitchen first! I don't control where the fruit flies go!"

"Kenny, Listen..."

I leaned my head back on the couch. "What?"

"I spoke to the landlord while you were gone, and he's agreed to break your lease. I've decided you need to find another place to live. I'm sorry. I can't keep doing this anymore. I've tried to help, but I am not in a mental space to continue coming to bat for you. I will give you until the end of next month to find a new place to live."

The Devil Actually Wears Plaid

I was drunk the whole red-eye flight to Texas. I began the night by stopping at R Place for a few beers. I then downed a few more beers at a pub in the airport, followed by two shots of Tito's Vodka with a can of Bloody Mary mix while on the plane. I only had ninety dollars left after these alcohol splurges, still needed money for a new place to live, and payday was still two weeks away. Despite all of this, all I could think about was getting drunk again.

Earlier that afternoon at the gym, I had to swallow my pride and ask for help to make the trip to Texas work out.

"Hey, Sole? Can I share a hotel room with Amir and have the gym pay for my Uber to and from the airport this weekend?"

I framed my financial struggles as saving up for a new place to live because I had to leave the Hobbit Hole at the end of the month. While it was true I couldn't afford the relocation costs, what I neglected to inform Sole was the fact I had successfully squandered each paycheck on adult beverages. I was living way beyond my means. Was this rock bottom?

Sole checked her phone, "What time do you get in?"

"Well—"

I touched down in Dallas-Fort Worth around 5:00 a.m. Still drunk, I walked around the airport in a haze. I'd need to be sober in time for the open training session in just a few hours. Should I skip the training and hope for the best when I compete? I sat in a Burger King in time for breakfast to give Sole more time to sleep before bothering her for an Uber. After placing my order, I checked my balance and noted I had $79 to carry me through the next two weeks. Had I frivolously spent everything on getting wasted? I became a frantic bank account checker. I'd need to be devoted to frugality on this trip. I called Sole around 6:30 a.m. so she could call me an Uber to the hotel, almost forty-five minutes away.

Amir woke me from my nap, the humble beginnings of a hangover taking root. My head pounding, my body feeling sluggish. "Grab some water and a quick bite to eat. Training starts in ten minutes!"

I grumbled, "Do I have to?" covering my face with a pillow.

"Only if you want practice time on the equipment."

"Fuck," I sat up in my bed. "Okay... I'm getting dressed."

The arena felt freezing. Two Skakun Rod floors sat right next to each other, with roughly thirty feet of space between for coaches to meander back and forth in the event of multiple athletes competing simultaneously. Across the arena from the rod floors sat four Gaofei Trampolines, where gymnasts jumped while their coaches stood beneath, ready to catch anyone who might fly off.

Two double mini trampolines sat on the outer edge of the arena. The competition floor lay on top floorboards covering an ice rink.

"That's why it's so cold in here." I protested to Sole, who bundled up in her jacket. "How do they expect us to compete here when it feels like a literal freezer?"

Sole crossed her arms, "Just go warm up and you'll do fine! You've got this Kenny! Think positive!"

The rod floor had brand-new carpet-bonded foam on top; running and initiating a round-off felt slippery. One of the girls from a different club agreed. "It feels like we're being forced to tumble in the snow!"

I walked over to Sole, ready to spread negativity, "I'm not going to be able to compete on this floor. It isn't anything like our floor at home!"

"Kenny. You'll be fine."

"No, I won't."

"You have a whole hour to feel out the equipment. Just warm your body up; you've done this pass a thousand times before. You've got this! Just believe in yourself, okay?"

I stood beside the rod floor runway. "I'd rather tumble on the summit floor at this point. There's no way. Everything feels off."

"I don't know what to tell you other than I believe in you. You are strong and more than capable of doing this!"

I felt weak, out of shape, and slightly wobbly. I convinced myself I felt this way because I hadn't had much time to train back home—being hungover had nothing to do with my performance. I wallowed in self-doubt, but Sole maintained an empathetic and encouraging line of communication.

"Kenny," She looked at me and said, "I really believe in you. You can do this!" as I took to the floor behind four other gymnasts.

Kacy, a coach from Tennessee, stood off in the distance, coaching her athletes. As I began warming up my tumbling passes, Kacy introduced herself to Sole. Kacy had long blond curly hair and a southern draw when she spoke. I didn't hear what they said, but Kacy pulled me aside when I returned from the landing deck. "Listen here. When you step out onto THAT FLOOR, you are competing. This is a pressure situation, and YOU ARE COMPETING. Do you understand me? Now I am going to have Zeke stand at the end, and you will put your double back dismount into your pass!"

Zeke? Who is Zeke?

Zeke was a tall, stark black man with an easy-going yet all-or-nothing demeanor. Even with him standing in to spot me, I didn't put the double back tuck into my tumbling pass. He pulled me aside. "Look, you've obviously had a night out. I can smell it on you. You can't train while you're impaired like this, are you crazy?"

"I'm not drunk, I'm just a little hung over."

"Same thing kid. Look, I'll help you put your passes together when you go to compete. Do you know which day you will compete?"

"Tomorrow morning."

"Perfect. Go get some sleep and lay off the booze until after you compete, got it?" He walked away but then stopped and looked back in my direction. "Hell, I'll even buy you a couple of drinks if you nail your routine!"

He didn't have to tell me twice. I walked back to the hotel, drank water, and napped.

The following day, Zeke stood at the end of the rod floor, halfway on the end deck. Did I feel well-rested and ready to compete? Sole and Kacy stood closer to staging, where all the athletes

sat in foldout chairs. I stood fourth in line and only had three practice passes on the equipment before I'd compete. I ran through
the more difficult of my two tumbling passes for my first warm-up
and failed the dismount by only throwing a layout instead of the
double-back tuck. "Look, if I'm standing here, it's all or nothing,
kid. You need to throw the double back. It's as simple as that."

I walked back to the staging area. Kacy had more words for
me, "You need to decide whether you're going to commit to your
tumbling pass. If you're going to do it, then do it! If not, then don't
even bother going!"

I looked at Kacy and Sole. "Look, I can't do this. I'm a failure."

"You are not, and you can!" Sole said. "You can because I've seen
you do this hundreds of times before. Now go out there and show
'em who's boss!"

Kacy pulled me aside again, "Zeke is standing at the end ready
to spot. All you gotta do is compete like you know how!" then she
walked off to the side with Sole.

All or nothing, I said to myself.

The judge saluted, and I saluted back. I ran across the
floor—Round-off, *whip, whip, whip, whip, back handspring, back
handspring*. I set up into the air and felt my body move into au-
topilot. Instinctively, I pulled my legs into a tucked position and
rotated twice. I could see the yellow landing deck in the air, and
then I landed on my feet. In the distance, I could hear spectators
cheering. Were they cheering for me? Did the spectators realize I
had been struggling yesterday and today? Zeke patted me as we
walked back toward Sole and Kacy. "I owe you a shot, kid."

"Atta boy, Kenny!" Kacy came over and hugged me.

Sole Joined in. "See. I told you so!"

I noticed that the corrections Zeke and Kacy gave me all weekend were those Sole gave me during practice at home. Maybe I did have much to learn from Sole after all.

Back in Seattle, I never realized how much fun gymnastics could be with Sole as my coach. We continued to build off Whitaker's foundation, and the results were phenomenal. She taught me how to throw a double-twisting double back. She also developed my first double layouts. The love I experienced for gymnastics returned, and I began to believe I did stand a chance to go elite in power tumbling.

Sole invited me to travel to Louisiana for a weeklong Trampoline and Tumbling clinic at two gyms, one in New Orleans and the other in Lafayette. Whitaker scheduled the trip before his resignation. Now that he no longer lived in Washington, this allowed me to travel with Sole. The gym flew us out, each with a couple hundred dollars per diem for our travels.

"Where's the first gym?" I asked on our way into the hotel.

"I'm checking the itinerary," Sole scrolled through her emails. "But the only gym listed is Trampoline and Tumbling Express in Lafayette."

I looked at Sole with a raised eyebrow, "So, then we're just getting a paid three-day vacation in New Orleans before driving out to a gym a couple hours away?"

"I mean, the hotel is already booked; we aren't the ones who booked it. I won't say anything if you don't?"

"My lips are sealed!" I added, "Also... Do you think we'll see any alligators while we're here?"

After a short pause, she shrugged her shoulders.

We spent our unplanned vacation like a couple of tourists. We wandered the streets and visited Cafe Du Monde. We ordered Starbucks and McDonald's and noted how neither establishment smelled like a Starbucks or McDonald's, but more like stagnant soapy water and a hint of bleach or maybe an old school house. In the mid-afternoon, we took a nap before returning to the streets.

"That guy just got held up at knife point!" Sole said, pulling me toward her.

Not too long after that, a drug dealer tried selling us crack. "Uh, run away!" Sole belted, and then we ran back toward the hotel.

I got drunk ordering Hurricanes from Pat O'Briens and experimented with the gator bites. "Umm they're kinda chewy. I'm not sure how I feel about these." I said, then sipped the Hurricane to wash it down. "I don't think gator bites are for me."

We wandered like buffalo through Bourbon Street, popping our heads in the next bar, boasting loud music and merry people. We received Mardi-gras beads while chatting up bartenders and other tourists. I cooed at overtly friendly pigeons, hoping that I could pet them like a dog. By nightfall, we stopped at a Walgreens to grab a couple of cheap liquor bottles to pregame before heading out into the night.

We probably stopped into every bar in sight. We later met up for dinner with a friend of Sole's who lived in the area, then made our way out to a jazz bar, where I became increasingly tired and drunk.

"Call me an Uber!" I demanded. "I'm going back to the hotel, now!"

"Chill out, let's stay a while longer."

"No! Call me an Uber now!" I yelled.

"Okay, okay, sheesh. Hold on."

I woke up a few hours later, still drunk, to Sole and her friend entering the room.

"Oh my God, I'm so happy you're back!" I perked up.

Instead of returning to bed, we played music and threw backflips on the mattress. Sole's friend broke the entire bed frame, and we had to jerry-rig it back together before calling it a night. The hotel never noticed. In the morning, Sole drove us across I-10.

"Alligator!" She screamed.

"Where?" I frantically searched left and right.

She laughed, "Made you look."

A state trooper pulled us over for speeding less than a second later. "This would happen here." She announced, sinking into her seat. We never did encounter any free-roaming alligators.

After moving out of the Hobbit Hole, I settled into a micro-studio apartment just off 13th and John Street in Capitol Hill, a few blocks away from the north end of Cal Anderson Park. I now lived within walking distance of all the gay bars in the area. One Saturday night, I stood in line at the new gay bar in the neighborhood to order a cocktail. I locked eyes with this incredibly handsome, tall, muscular, and hairy-chested bartender slinging drinks shirtless. As he came out of the back to return to his well, he propped right next to the bartender serving my line. He leaned in next to her, kept his gaze on me, and then pointed at me to exit the queue and come forward. This Godly figure was summoning me to him.

Uh.

I pointed at myself, and the bartender shook his head and said, "Yes, you! What are you drinking?"

I yelled across the loud music, "Sex on the Beach! But I just cut all these people!"

He looked me up and down. "Yeah, I don't care."

As I walked away, cocktail in hand, one of the guys who stood ahead of me in line said, "I think that bartender likes you!"

I sipped the red drink, "Do you really think so?"

"His well is literally on the other end of the bar. He likes you." He nudged me in his direction. "Go talk to him!"

I spent the rest of my night ordering cocktails from the bartender; he said his name was Brandon, and he added me on Snapchat.

The following Monday afternoon. I walked through the gym and up the stairs into the coach's offices to prepare for my day. I sat down and logged into the computer to write down the names of the students I was teaching for the day. I could see Sole walking up the stairs through the window before she opened the door. "Jillian and I need to have a meeting with you and Amir in the conference room."

"Are we in trouble? What's going on?"

I walked into the conference room upstairs, looked at the table, and saw Amir sitting beside Jillian. Sole sat and then dropped a bomb. "I am leaving King County Gymnastics! I have accepted a position at USA Gymnastics and will relocate to Indianapolis in two weeks!"

"Two weeks? What about the State Meet? And Regionals or Nationals?"

"I'm sorry to drop this bomb on you."

"Kenny," Jillian said. "We are currently interviewing with several candidates who might be able to jump in and take Sole's place. In the meantime, though, I'll need you and Amir to step up and coach at state this year. I'll be there to help support you the best I can."

Sole's announcement of her new job felt like another devastating blow. But I understood. Who could pass up an opportunity like this? Another coach leaving the gym would spring up as the next logical plot point in my storyline, but what could I do about it? I looked back at the events leading to this point and realized how helpful it was to have a coach believe in me. However, I could still succeed in training independently moving forward. I supported her decision to move on to preponderant opportunities—she deserved it. I felt grateful for the chance to be coached by her, even if only briefly. She contributed to an immense amount of personal growth, professionally and athletically. On her final day at the gym, I let her know how grateful I was for her in my life. She echoed the same.

Amir drove us forty-five minutes south to Summit Gymnastics on the morning of the State Championship meet. It was our first gymnastics meet without Sole. We were now the interim head coaches for the trampoline and tumbling team. Jillian also met us on the competition floor.

"How are you this morning?" I asked her as she rocked back and forth from her heels to her toes.

"I had a fun morning," she said, "I got a call last night around two in the morning from the security system urging me to go check out the gym. When I arrived, there was a naked man running around and peeing all over. He also tore our billboards off the walls. And then when the police arrived, they just watched him run around and pee everywhere!"

"Uh..." I said, trying hard to hold in my laughter. "I'm sorry, I shouldn't be laughing right now."

"I asked the officers if they were going to apprehend him, and they just looked at me and laughed and said 'no.' It took them forty-five minutes to get him into custody."

"Wait for real?"

"Yeah. The guy was drunk. He spent nearly twenty minutes prying the door to the gym open."

I laughed again but felt terrible.

"Anyway, I'm not staying the whole day, I just wanted to come and show up for support to see if either of you two needed anything?"

"I think we're good!"

"Alright. Have a good competition and take lots of pictures!" Jillian said and then drove home.

The state championship meet was exhausting. I wasn't hungover before competing this time, though. I learned that lesson in Texas. Compete first, drink later. All three state championship meet sessions took place in one day, so we were at the gym well into the evening after the sunset. Before I competed, I thought about everything that happened till now. By now, I should have been competing as an elite-level power tumbler instead of level 10. I reflected on the pain I experienced as a kid who wanted to be in gymnastics. So often, I got labeled gay, and not in an empowering, fun way. But in the degrading what-the-fuck-is-wrong-with-you type of way. I had to fight my way into this sport.

Before Sole moved, she hinted that King County Gymnastics recruited Neil Hahns as head coach. But right now, everyone was still intricately gridlocked into a hectic meet season. Nobody had wiggle room to make a drastic decision on such short notice. I only remember a little of the state championship. It's all a blur, but I must have done well because King County Gymnastics flew me to Las Vegas the following month to coach and compete at the regional championships. At the end of the state meet, I sat on the floor next to Amir while the final session's award ceremony was underway.

We both looked up simultaneously and saw Neil hovering over us. "I'll see you guys on Monday."

I looked at Neil. "What's on Monday?"

"Work," he said, then Amir and I looked at each other.

On the car ride home, I lamented to Amir, "I can't believe they hired Neil."

He kept his eyes on the road. "I don't know. This could be good for us."

"Have you met the man? He has the personality of a brick!"

At first, Neil coaching in our gym felt similar to having the main antagonist from an iconic 2006 film (starring Meryl Streep and Anne Hathaway) as a gymnastics coach and boss. Most of the time, Neil was a man of very few words, but when he gave instructions, suddenly, he rambled the whole spiel about a premier New York photography studio and a famous French photographer. By that, I mean he spat lengthy verbal assignments at me in one breath, and I'd only digest the first couple of parts before not knowing what to do next. So, naturally, I kept spotting back handsprings with the younger kids.

He walked over to me about twenty minutes into the nebulous assignment. "Did they finish the assignment I gave you?"

"Not even close."

"Well hurry along, please."

Despite Neils' fast-paced nature, his guidance of the trampoline and tumbling program felt like the days Whitaker led it. Kids were making progress, and some of the original parents who had withdrawn their kids returned for the opportunity to train with Neil.

The weekend of Regionals, we flew into Las Vegas from Seattle a few days before the competition started. While the Seattle May weather still felt cold and rainy, Las Vegas felt like Summer. Neil needed to be in Vegas early to help set up since he worked as a judge. My first impression of Vegas was that I never wanted to return there. I loved the weather, but the vibes were interesting. Sidewalks seemed to morph into casinos, and cigarette smoke permeated every nook and cranny. There were also tons of half-naked women wearing elaborate headdresses passing out cards promoting strip clubs, even to the kids on gymnastics teams waiting with their parents in line to check in at the Westgate Hotel.

"Is that even appropriate?" I asked the mom behind me.

"I don't think so... but it's Vegas."

We promptly threw the cards into the trash can.

The competition was my final shot at qualifying for the National Championships in Milwaukee later that Summer. Neil had all but taken over as my coach. He mostly didn't seem to care, maybe because I didn't. Perhaps I didn't care because I knew I couldn't afford the trip to Milwaukee. When I looked to Neil for guidance, I assumed elite coaches had extensive and elaborate set-ups, stations, and drills to correct any problems commonly faced. Instead, he spoke more calculatedly, often making only minor corrections.

"Straighten your arms, Kenny."

I looked at him as if he had given me a complex formula. "How do I even begin to put that into practice?"

"I said what I meant. Straighten your arms."

Neil was simple and profound. Once I figured out the simple correction, my tumbling became more consistent. As a coach, Neil didn't need the bells and whistles to gain momentum from his athlete—just simplicity and an ability to listen. Though introverted and preferred to keep to himself, he had a quirky sense of humor once you broke through the facade. Once, I overheard his instructions for a recreational trampoline class.

"Listen. So. You're going to run. Straight jump. Tuck Jump, then dismount with a front tuck. Got it?" Neil then turned to one of the shy girls in his class. "Are those panda earrings, Jessica? Hailey doesn't have panda earrings like Jessica. Why doesn't Hailey have panda earrings, too?"

Was this his attempt to build a coach-athlete relationship that was light-hearted and, at times, silly? Other times, Neil would pick younger kids up—still standing—one hand holding their hands and the other holding their feet, and he'd walk them around the spring floor holding them up while they balanced. The kids seem to enjoy this maneuver. During his candid moments with the kids, I tried to build a rapport with him. "What's your favorite color?" I asked before remembering that he wasn't some five-year-old child.

"Plaid," he said without missing a beat.

When it came time to compete, I stuck my double-back tuck dismount and finished third place at the regional championships. I didn't care about the results, though. I couldn't afford the trip to Milwaukee for the USA Gymnastics Championships and wouldn't be going that year. King County Gymnastics only paid my way to Vegas for regionals because they needed me to help coach at the meet because of how many kids were in attendance. Neils's arrival at King County Gymnastics meant all his kids from his original gym joined our team. But not all of them would qualify for nationals. There would be very few who qualified for the USA Gymnastics Championships. King County Gymnastics wouldn't need me in Milwaukee as a third coach. I came for the free ride in Vegas, focused on getting drunk at Piranha Nightclub.

Piranha was unlike any other gay nightclub I'd ever been to, with three dancing rooms and the sexiest bartenders I'd ever seen. I wanted to be drunk and make out with the next available guy I met at the club. By this point, going out to gay bars with less than one hundred dollars in my bank account had become my standard. I only had around fifty dollars in Vegas when I walked to Piranha. After standing in line to get into the club for some time, I paid a hefty twenty-dollar cover charge, then skipped straight to the bar. "Can I get a Vodka Soda?"

"That'll be thirteen dollars!"

When the bartender returned my card with the receipt, he charged me twenty-six dollars instead of the thirteen dollars he quoted. I mentioned that my tab was supposed to be thirteen dollars. He looked at me and shrugged, "There's nothing I can do about this," then walked away.

I drank my twenty-six-dollar cocktail, feeling slighted by the bartender. That is until I noticed a cute guy looking at me. He got me drunk, we danced, swapped tongues, then eventually returned to his hotel at the Luxor, where we fucked for several hours into the early morning. I only had a few dollars in my account after the night out, not nearly enough to cover the Uber charge from the Luxor back to the Westgate Hotel. We finished around five a.m. I called an Uber, hoping the request wouldn't get declined.

Thankfully, it didn't. But I overdrew my bank account.

Paradigm Shift

After returning to the gym from my long weekend in Las Vegas, I welcomed a gaggle of eleven-year-old kids in my trampoline class, who immediately began asking me personal questions. "Coach Kenny?" One of the boys sitting before me asked.

"What's up EJ?"

He sat down in a piked position. "Why did Coach Jackie kick you out of her apartment?"

I sat there for a moment in disbelief. Who told my students this information? I tried to play it off. "I wasn't kicked out of anywhere." I felt like my brain was short-circuiting.

EJ brought forth his curiosity with an outright jolly smile drawn on his face. "Does coach Jackie not like you anymore? Why did you get kicked out?"

I continued sitting, shocked, trying to process everything I was hearing. "This didn't happen, and Coach Jackie and I are still friends."

The reality was that Jack and I were still not friends. We hadn't spoken in months.

"We want to know why coach Jackie kicked you out!" He continued badgering me, putting his left leg out to slide into a split.

"Okay friends!" I snapped. "This conversation is now over!"

I continued stretching the class when the girl beside EJ began asking questions. "Have you ever been drunk before? I heard you get drunk like a lot!" She giggled with EJ.

"Listen up! This is not a conversation we will be having together. I don't know where you're getting this information, but it's going to stop here!"

Incensed and now grappling with plummeting self-esteem, I sent Jack a text message.

> Jackie! Why are you telling my students about our private affairs?

What are you talking about?

> You know what I'm talking about! My students found out everything that happened!

That's weird, but I didn't say anything to them. You know I would never do that!

> Okay, if you didn't, who did? Because it wasn't me!

I'm on a date right now, but come over this weekend, and let's talk about it. I know who started this.

> Who?

James.

I spent the next few days pondering how James would know, and then it hit me. While Jack and I were fighting, James swooped in as her go-to friend.

I climbed the stairwell leading into Jack's new apartment in Greenwood. She stood between her kitchen and living room, uncorking a bottle of wine.

"Here. It's 14 Hands," she said, handing me a brown sloth coffee mug. We nested into her oversized bean bag chairs. "Well, I mean it would make sense. We were hanging out and talking about the whole ordeal, right as it happened. James would be the only one privy to this information."

I kept looking at her ceiling, "He's an idiot! Like I can't even!"

"Well, if it makes you feel any better, I've had to cut him out of my life."

I sat up, "Wait, what? Shut up!"

"Yeah, he has a lot of deep issues I don't have the bandwidth for."

I wanted to know more. "How so?"

"Well, he's manic for one. A few nights ago, I came over to his apartment and he had busted out all his windows, threw his television out of the window and proceeded to cut holes into his clothing as I entered the apartment. I called the police and had to tell him to seek professional help because I am not equipped to deal with his situation."

"Oh my God! Seriously?"

"Yep. Other things happened, but it wouldn't be right for us to discuss it."

We sat in silence, sipping our sloth wine. "What are you going to do about this?"

I swirled the wine around the mug and watched as a few deep red drops sloshed onto my sweater. "I'm going to talk to Jillian and schedule a meeting with Human Resources, and hopefully be taken off these classes."

"Good idea."

The wine continued to flow, and I could feel myself slip into a sentimental buzz. "I'm glad we could remain friends despite the chaos of the last few months."

Jack held out her glass to cheers.

"Friends?"

"Friends!"

Clink! (This cliched moment most certainly didn't happen. But for narrative sake, we made up.)

At some point in the evening, our conversation shifted toward religious trauma. Jack was the person I felt most comfortable being raw about the battle between my sexuality and opposing faith. She was like my water bottle girl—the person sitting outside the boxing ring while their person goes in to fight. As I boxed my faith, she had a towel and water bottle ready, literally and metaphorically.

You're drunk. Have some water! She'd often say.

No! I only drink alcohol! I'd say back.

One time, while I blacked out at a house party, Jack spun my water intake as a challenge, "I bet you can't drink all this water!" She dared. Then I drank the water while everyone yelled, "*Chug! Chug! Chug!*"

I was still spiritually struggling. I wanted to flip a switch and permanently turn it off. Jack was like my part-time, unqualified therapist. I vented everything about my life to her. Jack never confirmed or denied my convictions. She knew better than to add fuel to this fire, or maybe she didn't know how to respond.

"So, where do you think all this originates?" she asked.

"When I was a kid, I got in trouble—a lot. I am trying to remember the specifics of this day. Both my parents were visibly upset at whatever I did, maybe I stole something or got caught playing with fire. They were so upset at me that they came into my bedroom and removed everything. They emptied my closet, took the linens from my bed, and hauled my dresser and toys out of the bedroom into the basement. Not long after all that, Dad came in and told me to strip out my clothes. 'This is for your own good, son!' he said as I cried, begging him to let me keep my clothes on."

Jack had tears welling in her eyes as the story unfolded.

She told me this was child abuse. I thought she was exaggerating. There was no way my experiences had been child abuse. I had never told anybody that story. I felt almost ashamed even when discussing it.

"Later," I continued, "my neighbors came up to the porch and tapped on my window to see if I could come out and play. Dad caught me peeking out of the blinds and he barged into my room. 'if you open those blinds again, I will duct tape the window from the outside so you can't peek out!'"

"That's psychological abuse," Jack added.

I tried to defend my parents, letting her know these types of punishments weren't a daily occurrence; my punishments always resulted from my poor decisions. I only had myself to blame.

"It doesn't mean it wasn't child abuse."

Were my parents bad people?

"Your parents were trying to do the best they could with the situation. Kenny, it's okay to admit their best wasn't enough."

I had never taken inventory of my childhood the way I was now, unpacking and viewing it differently. Was it child abuse? Was the deep shame I felt being shirtless in front of others related? Was this why I wet the bed every night until middle school? Dots were connecting. Jack concluded our night by telling me she wasn't a therapist.

"The only thing I will say," she said, "is my therapist once told me the things we go through in childhood often come back uglier in adulthood."

She was right.

The rain fell against the window of my apartment. I paced back and forth, thinking about my life and all the decisions I made along the way. Why did I leave the church if I would land right back where I started? My determination to become a disciple always originated from my beliefs about myself and the world around me. Maybe I did undergo a classic case of brainwashing. The day I left the church, the sentiment had always been: *when will I go back to church?* I never questioned the ICOC's theology. I lived each day thinking I was a dead man walking. Somedays, I wanted the strength and courage to walk away from the LGBTQ community in pursuit of righteousness so I could once again have the hope of Heaven. But most of the time, I wanted to be loved. Where was God in all of this?

I would be miserable as a disciple but desolate if I abandoned this small piece of my identity. Panic attacks over my salvation and the conflicting lifestyle I swam in became more frequent. Several years had passed since I withdrew my membership from the International Churches of Christ, yet I still felt brainwashed. I routinely tricked myself into thinking I was free from the church's clutches, but the church held me captive as a member, and the church still held me captive even now. Things were so bad that I thought the only way to exist within myself was by snorting lines of cocaine and binge drinking.

Joining a different church never even crossed my mind. In my mind, I viewed the ICOC as the only church that taught the true Gospel. I had doubts about my ability to be righteous, but I never wavered in the convictions brought about by my faith in the ICOC; I only slapped a booze-infused band-aid on them. What if everything the church taught me was a lie? What if the organization I participated in was precisely that—a four-letter word mentioned in a Barbara Walters interview? I couldn't grasp the possibility maybe the church was a purveyor of falsehood and botched theology. Perhaps I didn't want to understand fully. Still, had I been duped?

I ordered a book detailing the organization's departure from the authentic Gospel message. The author had once been a member of the ICOC. I almost felt afraid to start reading. For one, the book had too many pages, but did I have the capacity to discover a truth if it didn't fit my perception? Not knowing was exhausting. I took a deep breath and reflected for a moment. If this were true, it would set me free. But if it were false, it would only strengthen my faith, perhaps even give me the courage to return—but for real.

Over two weeks, I went on the journey of a lifetime. I had never experienced the feeling of internal freedom so vehemently. The author presented the Gospel in a way I never understood before. He confirmed that ICOC doctrines were a false legalistic gospel front-loaded with works. I never understood what Christians meant when they said they were "saved by grace through faith." I only understood what the organization taught me regarding salvation. I needed to become a disciple, as defined by the ICOC. I needed to confess every single sin each day. Baptism was the essential work paving the way for salvation. The church and its organization had a long list of do's and don'ts that members must strictly follow to be considered faithful to Jesus. "Modern-day Pharisees," the author called the church members.

I recalled a sermon I sat in years earlier in church, "Only saved disciples are real Christians. Disciples of Jesus are God's chosen flock. It's the man who sharpens his brother who earns his ticket to Heaven."

What I began learning about faith and grace was opposite to the "do it yourself" Gospel, underwritten as my knowledge's default. In the ICOC, I had to do everything for God so that He would love me. But this Gospel seemed to be genuine and attainable. I couldn't become what the ICOC wanted me to be because they built their system on legalism instead of grace.

I dropped my phone—the proverbial mic-drop to the battle I'd fought. Then, I stood to look out the window overlooking John Street. The rain settled, and the sun peered through a sliver in the clouds over the Seattle Sound. Everything seemed vibrant. How could I have not known sooner? How could I have been so stupid not to realize that I had fallen into a spiritual rat race? How did I not see the signs earlier? Each time I learned more of the truth regarding the organization, thought reform techniques the ICOC taught me grounded me right back into the system. What frustrated me most was the feeling of being gaslit by members into thinking the organization's label by outsiders as a cult was an empty form of persecution they had to endure. The whole time, I could have freed myself from this horror but instead struggled to find my true identity. All that time I considered myself a member of the Queer community at the time, I had beliefs opposed to it. But that was all changing.

After unpacking the toxic beliefs, I was ready to move on with my life. I needed to figure out where to start. Would I need to find a separate belief system? What would it be exactly? Would I need a therapist? Was it okay to admit that I didn't know? Did I even need to know all the answers to life's most challenging questions? I thought about taking a personal hiatus from religion altogether. I began chipping away at the top of the iceberg. The author helped me dismantle several years of religious indoctrination throughout the two weeks I spent reading the book.

My feelings were erratic. I felt relieved and spirited one moment, then irrational, and lacked energy the next. But something uncanny happened to me. I could see in living color. I began to heal deep within, no longer subjected to a fearful or uneasy feeling any time I confronted my LGBTQ identity. My freedom was something worth celebrating. Still, I felt empty inside, like there was something else I needed to accomplish to finally feel whole.

Finding My Way

I was twenty-three when I qualified to compete at the USA Gymnastics Championships in Milwaukee, Wisconsin. At the regional championships in Las Vegas two months earlier, I only set out to earn a qualifying score. Since Neil and Amir were both coaching the optional team, none of the athletes I coached would be attending nationals. King County Gymnastics would only need those two to coach in Milwaukee. Additionally, I still felt that my circumstances weren't getting better. They were getting worse, and it was all my fault.

Sure, I had deconstructed my faith, but this didn't change the fact I still had insurmountable debt from years of night clubbing and financial mismanagement. I maxed my credit cards out. I had an overdue Money Tree loan, six outstanding four-hundred-dollar competition fees owed to King County Gymnastics, and an additional five hundred dollars of debt to an app allowing me to access my paycheck early. Now, I had to depend on it to survive. Initially, the app arrived as a godsend, but now it was a thorn in my side. I didn't know how I was staying afloat. The national championships were two weeks away, and I didn't have enough money to cover my airfare, let alone my hotel expenses. I wouldn't be competing. What was there to do now? I couldn't even afford to get drunk.

The truth is, my life did start looking up. I stood in the gym's lobby, chatting with parents as my students got their socks and shoes back on. *All These Things That I've Done* by The Killers played over the loudspeakers as my coworkers began their cleaning assignments for the evening.

Jillian approached me after I said goodbye to my students around 8:15 p.m.

"Could I have a word with you for a minute?"

"What's up?"

"I wanted to check in with you. How are you doing?"

"Okay, I guess."

"I want you to know how grateful I am for your sacrifice for the T&T program this year."

I told her it was no problem.

"This program," she said, "wouldn't have stayed afloat if it weren't for you and Amir. I noticed you had six overdue competition fees. When Whitaker put you on the team roster, the system must have automatically put you on a payment schedule. Whitaker didn't intend for you to pay those fees. So, I've cancelled the debt."

I gasped. "Wait, what?"

"I am also including you as a coach at nationals this year."

"Wait... Stop. So, you mean—"

"Yes," she smiled. "You'll be flying out to Milwaukee with a per diem for the week. You can go as a coach, and since you'll already be there, I want you to compete. You've earned it."

I was speechless.

Jillian walked back to her office, and I sat there in silence, taking in the moment as the song continued playing.

Amir and I rode the Bolt Bus from Seattle to Portland, Oregon. Why didn't we fly out of Seattle? I'm not sure, but we made the most out of it. We spent the afternoon roaming around the city—a street fair, Powell's Bookstore, and challenging a couple of drunk girls to a handstand walk-off in the middle of the bar at Buffalo Wild Wings. Portland was vibrant and seemed to parallel Seattle in many ways. We only had a few hours before arriving at the airport. We hopped onto the MAX Light Rail, thinking it would be a quick trip like it was in Seattle. The train moved slowly and stopped for ten minutes, so we decided to hop off and call an Uber to get us there on time. We sprinted through the airport to get to TSA. The line stretched for miles, it seemed.

The TSA agent eventually scanned the ticket on my phone. "Sir. You need to see your airline's Customer Service Representative to get a paper ticket. It's not scanning, so I can't let you through."

"Oh, well could I cut the line since I already waited? My plane is taking off soon."

"No."

"I have my ticket here on my phone. I'm going to miss my plane if I have to get paper ticket!"

"Sir, this is not my problem."

I looked back at the line and saw it had become considerably longer. Then I looked at Amir, who looked unsure. I exited the queue and sprinted to customer service.

"Please, ma'am. My ticket couldn't be scanned, and I cannot afford to miss this flight!"

"Okay, sir, one minute, please." It felt like an eternity. "Here you are," she said. I grabbed the paper ticket and sprinted to the back of the line, frantically texting Amir, who made it to our gate.

> I'm not going to make it in time. The line is longer than earlier.

A few seconds later, my phone started to ring. Neil.

"Neil! They wouldn't let me through and I'm not sure what to do," my voice shook.

"It will be okay. Stay in the line and see if you can still time it. If not, everything will be okay. We will still get you here in time." It never occurred to me the club would have issued me a new ticket if I couldn't get through. I could only panic.

> They're closing the doors in ten minutes. I told them about the situation, but they said they could only hold the flight a few minutes over schedule to accommodate.

I began cutting the line and yelling about my predicament as I passed.

> I'm going through the TSA now. Tell them I am running!

"Please let me through! My plane is taking off in five!" I pleaded with TSA and the people before me. "I was already in line and on time, but got kicked out because they needed me to get a paper ticket. Please, I need to get through!"

"Let the guy through!" the group in front of me joined in the commotion.

TSA relented. I ripped off my jacket and shoes like a human tornado, tapping my feet in anticipation on the ground as I waited behind an elderly couple who strolled through security. "Oh Hank. I forgot to put my necklace into the bin," the wife said.

"Let me take it off you dear."

"Hank, I don't have time for you to fumble to get some stupid necklace off your wife!" I whispered loud enough for them to give me dirty looks. I pushed past them without considering my actions.

Sorry! I did not say.

I grabbed my jacket and shoes and sprinted for the gate—one shoe on my foot, one in my hand, and my coat under my arms while dragging my suitcase. Once I got to the gate, the attendant began closing the door.

"Wait for me!" I yelled.

"Oh, your friend told us about you."

"The last passenger has arrived," the blond TSA agent radioed. "Can we let him on still?"

"You're in luck. They didn't close the door yet. Right this way, Kenneth."

I sat down, breathing hard. Amir smiled. "Right on time."

At the Wisconsin Center, athletes had one hour of training on the equipment before the competition kicked off for the week. Sole was in attendance and engaged in her position at USA Gymnastics, running around and ensuring everything proceeded smoothly. She often sat perched in the judge's panel near the trampolines. I knew this because she sent a Snapchat video of me practicing one of my tumbling passes. Even though she no longer coached me, it felt like she did. Neil was a phenomenal coach, but we didn't have a history or connection yet. When it was time for me to compete, Sole came over while I warmed up my passes. Kacy trailed her to wish me luck. Sole's words were reassuring, "You already made it. Now all there is left to do is put everything you have on the competition floor."

Kacy, however, gave her typical brute-forced encouragement. She always seemed to have a way of pulling the fire out of her athletes, "You step out onto the floor and give it everything you have! Got it? Now go out there and crush it!"

Across the way, Whitaker stood adjacent to Neil. He walked over to me. "Hey, kid. I wanted to wish you luck. I know things didn't work out as we could have hoped, but you still made it here, and I'm proud of you. Now go out there and kick some ass!"

We exchanged a fist bump, and he walked into the distance to coach one of his gymnasts climbing onto the Trampoline. Neil spat a correction at me while Amir stood on the sidelines, filming me with my iPhone 6. I stepped onto the runway of the rod floor. The judge saluted me. The moment felt eerily similar to standing at the starting line of my high school cross country races. I closed my eyes. I could see the Mead High School cross country team to my left and North Central High School to my right. Would I stack up? Why was I even competing here today? Suddenly, I could hear Miss. Driscoll's voice is loud and clear.

Because no one else is.

I opened my eyes, and I returned a salute to the judge. I began sprinting across the floor as I had hundreds of times. Round off, five whips, one back handspring. Whip, whip, whip, whip, whip, back handspring, I blocked my feet into the floor and stood quickly in preparation for my double backflip. I speedily pulled my legs into a tuck position, hoping to find my feet. As much as I want to write how I perfectly landed the skill and took home the gold medal—I didn't. Not even close. After pulling my double back tuck, I didn't rotate enough. I landed short and fell forward, taking home a tenth-place finish.

This competition was about celebrating the fact that I showed up in pursuit of my childhood dreams. Did I feel disappointed? I did at first. Now, I look back and view my fall as a rite of passage. Though I never became an Olympian, I still achieved the same full-twisting double backflip I watched elite gymnasts from the 1990s compete in their floor routines. I accomplished what used to be a dream. If eleven-year-old Kenny knew that twenty-three-year-old Kenny would eventually compete at nationals and walk away with a tenth-place finish, he'd be proud of me. So, I allowed myself a moment to feel proud. Though I never became an Olympian, I gave gymnastics everything I had. Despite the ups and downs in the sport, I fought to the end.

I returned to Seattle to meet with Brandon, the hot bartender. We were forming a relationship of sorts. People speculated we were dating. I knew I wanted to be his boyfriend.

"Here," he said, sending me a text message.

"What's this?" I asked, looking at the black box on my phone screen.

"A little pick me up. Since I have the finances, I wanted to help you find some stability.

"Oh... Wow!" I said. I was stunned as I read the Apple Cash amount of two thousand dollars, enough to pay off my credit card debt and get me back on my feet. "How can I ever repay you?"

"We'll come up with a solution, but I hope to teach you responsibility. I like you and I want to do my part to help you learn and grow from your mistakes."

Despite my numerous fuckups, I was limping along in the right direction. A few weeks later, after a shift of Saturday morning preschool classes at the gym, I sat in the Ballard Mighty-O Donuts, sipping on an iced mocha with sugar falling into my lap from the vegan donut I was tearing apart. I reflected on the last eighteen years I had pursued gymnastics, whether real or otherwise imagined. I knew it was time for me to move on with my life. I took to Instagram to pen a farewell of sorts:

I've always been a dreamer and looked at the bigger picture of the future. When I was younger, I wanted to be an Olympian. I knew it was an unrealistic goal, but I didn't let the doubts get in the way and chased my dream relentlessly. There's a saying that goes, "Shoot for the moon; even if you miss, you'll land among the stars." I never went to the Olympics. But I did my best with what I had and came far as a gymnast, and I'm so proud of what I've accomplished in this sport. I am officially retiring from the competitive side of gymnastics, and I want to take some time to thank everyone who has been a part of this journey with me for the last 18 years. For the coaches in my life who have invested their time and energy in a crazy, sassy athlete like me, I am indebted. Today, my goals have shifted, and my dreams have evolved; a vision of what the future holds still shines as bright for me as it did when I was younger, wanting to compete in the Olympics. My journey in this sport is far from over. I still have a whole coaching career ahead of me, and I get to share my passion and energy with all my athletes every day, and the possibilities are endless. If there's one thing I've learned through all of this, it's okay to chase unrealistic dreams because life is a journey, and you never know where it will take you. Do it on purpose; chase the unrealistic because with a bit of faith, passion, and determination, incredible things will happen, and you'll be glad it did. I know I am.

I stood from the table, brushed the donut crumbs on my lap onto the floor, and walked outside. It was a beautiful Seattle summer day. Brandon sat on his motorcycle in front of the coffee shop. He tossed me a helmet and jacket. "Hop on."

"Where are we going?"

"You'll see."

We rode to the West Point Light House in Discovery Park and watched the sun set into the sound. Everything would turn out alright.

The author. San Jose, California. May 8th, 2019.

Epilogue

The ICOC taught me to "work out" my "salvation with fear and trembling." Upon my defection, I used drugs and alcohol to cope with the "fear and trembling" aspect of living in what I viewed as sin. Once I deconstructed those toxic beliefs, I felt the burden of the whole organization lift off my shoulders. I got sober on July 24th, 2022; life has never felt so vibrant since then. Today, I live free from the control of the church, alcohol, and illicit substances.

Strength and Weakness Ministries messed me up. Many former members widely regard it as conversion therapy. As a member, I got plugged into a small support group. Two of the men in the group agreed to disciple me long distance. One of the topics that frequently came up in our conversations was masturbation and pornography. They'd ask me if I masturbated the night before. If I answered yes, they'd probe further by asking whether pornography was involved or not.

One of those disciplers went on to explain that within the bounds of marriage, a disciple could use masturbation as a tool to reprogram their brain. The scenario, he said, would allow them to create an attraction toward their wife rather than another man. Strength in Weaknesses' sole purpose is to convince LGBTQ people like me that our identities require consistent efforts to change or repress them.

Recently, it came to my attention that the person known in the book as Disciple A. died by suicide. While I do not know the specifics of what led them to this point, I can't help but wonder whether this heartbreaking tragedy is the result of Strength and Weakness Ministries. There is nothing good that comes from an organization that councils a person to repress their sexuality and gender identity. My heart grieves for this person and their family. The ICOC and SIW have since scrubbed their websites clean of any mention of Disciple A. as the poster child of SIW.

As of the writing of this book, the International Churches of Christ, along with its founder and several prominent members within the organization and its carbon copy, the International Christian Churches (ICC), have been named in several lawsuits alleging the cover-up of child sexual abuse and human trafficking within its ranks.

Acknowledgements

Stefany Bryan. Author and Editor. <3

This book would not be possible without my dear friend Stefany Bryan, who helped oversee it to its completion. She spent countless hours reading, editing, and offering me constant feedback. Stefany is one of my favorite people, and you should totally follow her on Instagram: @stefanybryanmusic.

I want to thank my boyfriend, Brandon, for his edits and for encouraging me to keep writing even when I tried to give up (which was often).

Thank you to my dear friend Jackie McCartin for our interviews and for allowing me to write about our time together in the Hobbit Hole. Your friendship has contributed to significant growth in my life; I wouldn't be who I am today without you.

I want to thank my former mentor and boss, Sole. You inspired me a great deal, and I am grateful for the time we spent together, even if only briefly.

Rachael Herron published a book called Fast Draft Your Memoir. We have never met before, but her book (and the workbook, too) helped me piece my story together. So, Rachael, if you're reading this—thank you.

I am grateful to Bryce Bailey, whose creativity and community outreach inspire me daily.

Thank you, Briana Driscoll-Waldman, for your years as my cross country coach and to all of my former cross country coaches for teaching the value of hard work and "digging deep." I learned my most valuable lessons on the track.

I want to acknowledge the Rogers High School Gymnastics team circa 2009-2012 for allowing me to take up space on the team. (Kenisha sends her overflowing gratitude.)

Thank you, Kayla Kamerer, my former gymnastics coach at Rogers, for teaching me how to flip a Tsukahara on the vault. It was a defining moment in my gymnastics career—the only reason I continued training.

I'd like to recognize all the gymnastics coaches who have worked to help me fine-tune into the athlete I became.

I want to give special recognition to my cousins, Dakota Vails and Bailey Janda. You were both instrumental in helping me shape a more positive theological outlook. Without your biblical knowledge and advice, I might not be here today.

Lastly, thank you to my family: my mom, my dad, my brother, and my sister, for helping shape me into who I am today.